Evangelizing the Cults

How to Share Jesus with Children, Parents,
Neighbors, and Friends
Who Are Involved in a Cult

WITHDRAWN

Edited by
Ronald Enroth

With best wishes,

VINE BOOKS

Servant Publications
Ann Arbor, Michigan

Vine Books is an imprint of Servant Publications especially designed to serve Evangelical Christians.

Passages from Scripture used in this work, unless otherwise indicated, are taken from the Holy Bible, New International Version. Copyright © 1973, 1978, 1984, by International Bible Society. Used by permission.

Published by Servant Publications
P.O. Box 8617
Ann Arbor, Michigan 48107

Cover design by Gerald Gawronski

90 91 92 93 94   10 9 8 7 6 5 4 3 2 1

Printed in the United States of America
ISBN 0-89283-671-7

Library of Congress Cataloging-in-Publication Data

Evangelizing the cults : how to share Jesus with children, parents, neighbors, and friends who are involved in a cult / edited by Ronald Enroth.
    p.   cm.
Includes bibliographical references.
ISBN 0-89283-671-7
  1. Cults—United States—Controversial literature.   2. Evangelistic work—United States.   3. Witness bearing (Christianity)
4. Christianity and other religions.   5. United States—Religion—1960-
I. Enroth, Robert M.
BL2525.E83   1990
248'.5—dc20   90-43128

Contents

Contributors

Mark C. Albrecht is a doctoral student at the University of Aarhus, Denmark, and has specialized in the study of Eastern religions. He is the author of *Reincarnation*.

James A. Beverley is professor of theology and ethics at Ontario Theological Seminary in Ontario, Canada. He is the author of *Crisis of Allegiance: A Study of Dissent among Jehovah's Witnesses*. An ordained minister in the Canadian Baptist Federation, he specializes in the study of new religious movements.

Ronald Enroth is professor of sociology at Westmont College in Santa Barbara, California, and author of *The Lure of the Cults* and *Youth, Brainwashing, and the Extremist Cults*.

Gordon R. Lewis is professor of theology and philosophy at Denver Seminary. He is founder and president of Evangelical Ministries to New Religions. His many books include: *Confronting the Cults, Testing Christianity's Truth Claims, and Integrative Theology* vols. 1 and 2.

Robert Passantino and his wife, Gretchen, direct Answers in Action, an education-oriented ministry located in Costa Mesa, California. He and his wife cohost a popular radio talk show and have coauthored several books, including *Answers to the Cultist at Your Door* and *Witch Hunt*, an evaluation of contemporary evangelical discernment techniques in the light of Scripture.

7

Ruth A. Tucker is a professional writer and a visiting professor at Trinity Evangelical Divinity School in Deerfield, Illinois. She has written several books, including *Another Gospel, Daughters of the Church* (with Walter L. Liefeld), and *Guardians of the Great Commission.*

Kurt Van Gorden is the director of two missions dedicated to evangelizing cults—Jude 3 Mission in Orange, California and the Utah Gospel Mission. Established in 1898, the Utah Gospel Mission is the oldest ministry to cults in the United States. He has contributed research to four books by Walter Martin and is a respected consultant on cults and apologetics.

Wesley P. Walters is pastor of Marissa Presbyterian Church in Marissa, Illinois. He has studied the cults for over thirty years, lectured at several Evangelical seminaries around the country, and written numerous articles for Christian journals on the cults.

Karen Winterburn spent twelve years studying and practicing the occult before recommitting her life to Jesus Christ in 1985. Karen is currently the Director of Mt. Carmel Outreach: Chicago and Suburban Branch in the Chicago area, where she lives with her husband and four sons.

J. Isamu Yamamoto, formerly a book editor with *Christianity Today,* has researched and written extensively on cults and new religious movements. He is the author of *The Puppet Master,* which deals with the Unification church, and *Beyond Buddhism.*

Introduction

NORTH AMERICAN SOCIETY has become a spiritual supermarket, offering something for everyone, the seasoned shopper as well as the person who buys on impulse. At one point in our history, our religious heritage was fairly homogeneous. That is, despite our denominational differences, we could all identify with a common religious core, something we refer to as our "Judeo-Christian tradition." Even folks who did not attend church very often knew something about the religious consensus that constituted what is often called the "moral fabric" of our society. We were a "Christian nation."

The religious scene is now very different. We can no longer take for granted a Christian consensus and we can no longer assume that spiritual seekers will turn to "the church" in their search. For those experiencing spiritual hunger, today's world offers a religious salad, an alphabet soup consisting of New Age gurus, Eastern mystics, and self-improvement programs, as well as a confusing array of Christian-sounding groups all claiming to have Jesus on their team.

Cults and new religious movements have been the focus of serious study, ridicule, and amused disinterest. Television reporters representing the spectrum of CBS News to "A Current Affair" have reminded us that religious cults make for interesting copy. Academic scholars from a variety of disciplines have dissected and analyzed the new religious movements, and concerned parents have warned us about their destructive impact on families. Evangelical authors have produced an impressive list of books on cults, ranging from seemingly unending critiques of the New Age movement to insider accounts of the Jehovah's Witnesses.

9

So why another book on cults? First, a few comments about what the book you are now reading is *not* attempting to do. This is not an encyclopedic handbook on religious cults. It is not an exhaustive, in-depth survey of the beliefs and practices of all the cults and new religions that can be found in North America at the end of this century. It is not aimed primarily at the Christian cult-watchers who are actively engaged in commendable apologetic and educational ministries. They are already familiar with most of the content of this book.

All the contributors to this volume are Evangelical Christians. They not only are knowledgeable about cults, but they are also committed to helping the average Christian person understand something about the various manifestations of cultism in today's world so that we can all effectively communicate the evangel—the gospel—to people we care about, deeply. Biblical Christians should want to share their faith not only with the unchurched and the irreligious, but with those persons involved in groups and movements outside the parameters of orthodox, biblical faith. As one of the contributors to this volume, Wesley Walters, puts it, the good news does not belong exclusively to us—we also owe it to those caught up in cults.

The purpose of this book, then, is to assist serious, caring Christians to achieve a compassionate understanding of a sampling of contemporary cults in order to be better able to introduce people in those groups to Jesus our Lord. Whether across the sea or across the backyard fence, we must never forget that the gospel presentation is about a *person;* it is a message that proclaims that Jesus was God become a *man,* who was *crucified,* then *rose* from the grave and now *reigns.*

The cults which we discuss are all currently active throughout North America. Several are large and very visible, like the Mormons and the Jehovah's Witnesses. We decided not to present a chapter on Christian Science since the influence of that movement is declining. Instead, we offer a chapter on Unity School of Christianity, a group with roots similar to Christian Science and which reflects the growing interest in "mind science" or "religious science" emphases.

Scientology, along with Eastern and New Age groups, represents the "newer" religions to impact the West. Another new group, the

Unification church of Reverend Moon, is worldwide in scope and syncretistic in belief. We also include a chapter on the general topic of the occult because there seems to be a revival of interest in this area and because there is an occult connection in so many cultic movements.

Finally, we have included a chapter which draws our attention to the cross-cultural and international dimensions of cultism. Just as Christian believers in the West have historically been involved in and supportive of overseas or "foreign" missions, we must also be sensitive to the fact that cults are expanding their influence worldwide. The task of evangelizing the cults does not stop at our own borders.

THE SCOPE OF THE TASK

It is important to begin by introducing basic terms, especially the word "cult." It is a term that means many things to many people. For many readers, it probably has derogatory or pejorative connotations. That is, it often conveys a negative image about the group under discussion.

Journalists and other popular writers usually describe "cults" in sensational, sometimes exotic, contexts. While *some* cults *sometimes* engage in behaviors that are unusual or bizarre when compared to more conventional religious groups, it is not our purpose here to focus on the more sensational aspects of cultic movements. We do not intend to be demeaning or derogatory when we use the word cult. Members of religious cults are usually no different from our next-door neighbor or our colleagues at work. Christians should be especially sensitive to the problem of contributing to unfair stereotypes.

For the purposes of this book, we define the word "cult" to mean a group of religious people whose belief system and practices deviate significantly from and often contradict the Holy Scriptures as interpreted by orthodox, biblical Christianity and as expressed in such statements as the Apostles' Creed. In short, this theological definition of cult focuses attention on the truth claims of any given group and compares them with the infallible Word of God, the Bible.

Such an approach requires making judgments about "true"

teaching and "false" teaching, distinctions that are unimportant to secular observers and which, in fact, often elicit charges of narrow-mindedness and even religious bigotry. Evangelical Christians must hold to the conviction that the Bible serves as the only baseline for comparison when making determinations of truth and error, even if such a position invites accusations of closeminded-ness. In a powerful essay on the tragedy of Jonestown, Stanley Hauerwas argues that Jim Jones' success represents a judgment on the church and on our society for providing people with so little religious content that they were unable to recognize heresy when they saw it. "A people who have lost any sense of how religious traditions are capable of truth and falsity can easily fall prey to the worst religious claims, having lost the religious moorings that might provide them with discriminating power."[1]

We live in a culture which often proclaims that all religions are equally valid and that there are many paths to the same truth. The basic ground rule in our pluralistic society is *tolerance*: thou shalt not judge another religion by your religion's standards. Hauerwas points out that sometimes even Christians are reluctant to pass judgment on religious phenomena on theological grounds for fear that such judgments might violate the norm of tolerance. "Like all good secularists, Christians today do not condemn the beliefs of cults but rather criticize them only for practices that seem to violate people's autonomy. After all, beliefs are a matter of personal choice, not subject to claims of truth or falsity. Only actions can be condemned and those only on a basis that is shared by our general culture."[2]

It is the conviction of the contributors to this book that, ultimately, any understanding of cultic systems necessarily requires examination of truth claims. Psychological and sociological explanations alone, as important and as helpful as they may be, fail to fully explain the destructive elements in cultism. For example, secular observers have noted that cults practice thought reform and often engage in recruitment practices which involve coercive persuasion. But the issue for the Christian, ultimately, is not whether the methods of converting are coercive, but whether what the converts are asked to believe and do is true.[3]

Some readers may question the appropriateness of including chapters on Buddhism and Hinduism in a book dealing with cults.

After all, are they not both considered to be world religions, along with Christianity, Judaism, and Islam? They are indeed world religions, but our concern here is primarily with the Hindu and Buddhist communities in North America whose influence has been considerable since 1965 when President Lyndon Johnson rescinded the Oriental Exclusion Act, unleashing a massive Asian immigration and setting the stage for the importation of many new religions and gurus from the East. "The United States and the West are experiencing a large-scale movement of both people and religion from East to West, a movement with the potential to remake the Western religious scene as significantly as the nineteenth-century Christian mission remade Africa and the Orient."[4] There are several dozen Buddhist temples in the greater Los Angeles area alone. And, as the chapter on the New Age movement will demonstrate, the impact of Eastern mysticism on New Age thinking is enormous.

Non-Christians and even some individuals within the Evangelical community are sometimes surprised to see Mormons included in the category of cult. "Many can understand why a Buddhist group or a Hindu sect differs from the Christian faith, but some think that Baptists, Presbyterians, and Mormons are all pretty much alike." Are the Latter-day Saints (Mormons) just another Protestant denomination? As you will discover when you read the chapter on Mormonism, the Mormons are neither Protestant nor Christian, in the true sense of that word. If we expect to be effective witnesses to these folks, we need to clearly understand the differences.

Whatever the label we apply to those who worship at alternative altars, we need to recognize that the task of evangelism is simply the act of accurately and sensitively presenting the Christian faith to non-Christians in such a way that they can understand it, and hopefully, believe it. Evangelizing cults and new religions is, in a sense, becoming a missionary to the people next door. Karen Winterburn, in her chapter on the occult, reminds us that witnessing to an occultist is a lot like being a foreign missionary.

Ruth Tucker's chapter on confronting the cults cross-culturally is another important reminder that cultic activity is not confined to the United States and Canada. Mormons and Jehovah's Witnesses are among the fastest growing religious bodies in Latin America. Bob Passantino tells us that Jehovah's Witnesses, in fact, are active in two hundred twelve countries. They recently held a huge rally in Poland.

Whatever else the dramatic changes taking place in the Soviet Union and Eastern Europe may mean, one thing is certain. Cults and new religious movements are capitalizing on the new openness and rushing in to fill at least part of the religious vacuum. While Evangelicals rejoice over the exciting opportunities to share the gospel of Christ, the same religious freedom afforded to us is not going unnoticed by the cults. Consider the following report of the open door for witness:

> The chance is now at hand to witness to people in [the Soviet Union and Eastern Europe] who are searching for truth and value. . . . We have an unprecedented historic opportunity to nourish a hungry and grateful people with God's truth and love.[5]

That assessment was written not by a representative of Evangelical Christianity, but by a member of Reverend Moon's Unification church. Unificationist leaders recognize that as many Communist countries abandon Marxist ideology, they will be ready and eager to accept new ideologies, including Unification thought. The Moonies have been busy sending teams to Czechoslovakia, Poland, and Russia. They have cosponsored a conference with the Russian Orthodox church (held in Moscow, Oct. 28 to Nov. 1, 1989) on the theme, "The Trinitarian Basis of Christian Unity." A top official of the Unification church used the occasion to meet with the head of the Department of External Affairs of the Orthodox church in an attempt to convince him that "the Unification church is good, real, and true."[6]

Cults, especially the New Age variety, are taking much of the credit for the easing of world tensions and the hope of freedom and unity on the planet. The March 19, 1990 issue of *Time* magazine carried a two-page advertisement announcing the Maharishi's "Master Plan to Create Heaven on Earth." The ad attributed the new dawning of happiness, peace, and freedom in many countries to the "Maharishi Effect"—created by millions of people practicing the guru's own brand of Transcendental Meditation (TM).

Writing from the Unificationist perspective and making reference to that group's holy book (*Divine Principle*), a follower of Reverend Moon offers the following insight into current events:

Without studying the Divine Principle understanding of history and the forces at work in the Last Days, it must be impossible for most people to comprehend the dramatic and unprecedented daily headlines . . .[7]

Another disciple of Sun Myung Moon expresses gratefulness "to Rev. Moon for providing the vision and leadership which is now bringing about the unity of the entire world. We are . . . now seeing the results of Rev. Moon's prayers and work."[8]

THE NATURE OF THE TASK

The primary task of the Christian church is to proclaim the gospel, not to fight the cults. Too often evangelical zeal to convert cultists takes on the appearance of an anti-cult crusade. We want to stamp out Satan in the next three weeks. But we are not cult-busters; we are agents of reconciliation, bearers of good news to those who do not know Jesus our Lord.

The word *gospel* means "good news." This presupposes that there is also some "bad news," or at least some unsatisfactory situation that the good news addresses. The bad news, of course, is the human condition, our fallenness, our sinfulness. Many cults do not acknowledge human sinfulness or they redefine and reinterpret the concept of sin. I am reminded of an ad I once saw for the Vedanta Press and Bookshop in Hollywood, California: "It is a sin to call anyone a sinner. It is a standing libel on human nature. Vedanta does not believe in sin, only error, and the greatest error is to think you are weak."

The cults offer their own prescriptions for alleviating or rectifying human brokenness. The Moonies speak of "restoration," the TM devotees offer "enlightenment," and the Hare Krishnas chant their way "back to godhead." It is at this very point of striving that the Christian gospel separates itself from all other religious endeavors. For the good news of the New Testament is the proclamation that God has taken the initiative to reveal and disclose himself through the sacrifice of his Son on the cross. The gospel thus originates with God and is a uniquely divine message. It is not a product of philosophy and clever argumentation, but it is a forthright statement about human nature spoken from God's perspective, and embodies the final solution to the problems of evil, suffering, and death. It is not a mystical message of secret wisdom for an initiated few. The secret is out, Jesus Christ is Lord!

In the Epistles, a statement in 1 Corinthians 15 stands out as perhaps the best short definition of the gospel, the gospel we are called to share with cultist and non-cultist alike. This passage, which begins at verse three, is thought by many scholars to be one of the oldest formulations of the apostolic church, a sort of "mini-creed" encapsulating the gospel, which Paul quotes thus: "For I received what I passed on to you as of first importance: that Christ died for our sins according to the scriptures, that he was buried, that he was raised on the third day according to the scriptures, and that he appeared to Peter, and then to the twelve."

This mini-creed, this kernel, which forms the basis for all gospel presentations, is called the *kerygma*, a Greek word that refers to the *content* of the preaching. The basic first-century tract, if they had one, would probably have read something like this:

The age of fulfillment has dawned, as the Scriptures foretold. God has sent his Messiah, Jesus. He died in shame upon a cross. But God raised him again from the tomb, and he has exalted him at God's right hand. He now offers forgiveness of sins and eternal salvation. The proof of all this is the power of the Holy Spirit whose effects you can readily see. This Jesus will return again to judge at the end of history. Therefore repent, believe, and be baptized.

The real task of evangelism is to endeavor to make sure that our friends and relatives in the cults truly understand this message.

In addition to the basic goal of clearly communicating the gospel of Christ, we must know something about the people we are trying to evangelize. Gordon Lewis in his chapter on the New Age tells us that just as missionaries must be familiar with the culture and religion of the people they want to reach, we must also attempt to learn as much as possible about the cult or new religion we encounter. That does not mean we all must become cult experts. But if you don't take the time to look into the beliefs and practices of a group, the person you are trying to win over may interpret your ignorance as lack of respect.

As Kurt Van Gorden stresses in his chapter on Scientology, we must respect the right of members of new religious movements to believe and practice their religion. But, he adds, showing respect for the Scientologist does not mean that Scientology is true!

In his chapter on the Unification church, James Beverley mentions something that is essential for everyone who is interested in evangelizing the cults: recognition of the fundamental freedom of religion that should be accorded to all people, including cult members. Unfortunately, anyone who engages in a critique of a cultist's faith or who seeks to change that person's mind about allegiance to that false teaching is subject to the accusation of being intolerant and perhaps lumped with the "anti-cult movement." Even if the Christian is respectful, sensitive, and loving in his approach, cultists strongly resent anyone who represents a threat to their group. Nevertheless, we cannot shrink from identifying spiritual counterfeits. The Bible reminds us to "test the spirits to see whether they are from God" (1 Jn 4:1). I repeat here what I have stated elsewhere:

A negative evaluation of any given group does not mean a lack of commitment . . . to religious freedom and the right of any group to freely promote its beliefs. The United States has a rich history of religious diversity and, as a citizen and as a Christian believer, I am committed to the preservation of pluralism. . . . Negative evaluation is not a synonym for "attack" and opposing opinion should not be reinterpreted as "anti-religious" or cited as evidence of intolerance. . . .[9]

If, in your dealings with members of cults, you can communicate something of the essence of the above declaration and do so with integrity, you will have taken a major step toward defusing the claim that Christians are insensitive to issues of religious liberty.

The task of evangelizing the cults also includes the need to identify the reasons why people are attracted to cults. Later in this volume Kurt Van Gorden discusses four basic reasons why people join cults. It is important to remember that theological and doctrinal attractions are often secondary to personal and social reasons. People find cults appealing because the groups meet basic human needs: the need to be affirmed, the need for community and family, the need for purpose and commitment, the need for spiritual fulfillment.

The tragedy is that cults often exploit the significant human and spiritual needs that are going unmet in today's world. Cult adherents fall victim to authoritarian structures that fail to deliver on their promises. Youthful idealism turns into empty frustration in the face of a works-oriented salvation. Sincere devotion is transformed into blind obedience to a fallible human leader.

Karen Winterburn is correct when she observes that if our only focus as a witness is in the realm of ideas and beliefs, we will never reach the person. At the same time, if our witness is strictly relational, our cultic friend will never hear the truth that sets people free. Concerned love alone never saves a person.

THE CHALLENGE OF THE TASK

As we approach the task of evangelizing the cults, we must first examine our commitment to the truth of the gospel and to the authority of God's Word. Once we understand that the gospel is really true and stands up to the most difficult scrutiny, our own faith is enlarged and we become more eager to share the gospel. While God does not call us all to be cult specialists, he does call us to be well-informed, and we owe it to the cultists we meet to give them a complete and accurate transmission of the good news, as well as answers to their questions and objections. "Always be prepared to make a defense to any one who calls you to account for the hope that is in you, yet do it with gentleness and reverence" (1 Pt 3:15, RSV).

David Fetcho, cofounder of the Spiritual Counterfeits Project, reiterates that evangelism cannot be viewed apart from the qualitative whole of the Christian life. It follows that we must evangelize out of our discipleship, not merely out of our expertise on the cults.

We do not need a cult specialist to help us apply the Bible's teachings on evangelism. The current proliferation of para-church counter-cult organizations, while positive in many respects, is at the same time alarmingly indicative of a widespread insecurity among Christians about their discipleship which breeds their insecurity. If personal and corporate discipleship are fully operative, however, they become the basis which Christians can rely on for authentic verbal proclamation, rather than on the borrowed expertise of some cult-research organization.[10]

As you engage in your own authentic verbal proclamation to your friends, acquaintances, or family members who are in cults, keep in mind St. Paul's Mars Hill discourse (Acts 17:16-34) which, Gordon Lewis reminds us, is a model of cult evangelism. Following Paul's example, our message must be:

1. *Relevant.* It must be tailored to the concerns of twentieth-century people, but without compromising its integrity.

2. *True.* We must first be convinced of this before we can convince others.

3. *Persuasive.* We have a responsibility to proclaim Christ clearly and effectively, while at the same time always recognizing God's authorship of conversion. The message must be presented with the power of the Holy Spirit.

4. *Compassionate.* Gentle persuasion and an attitude of love and concern must characterize our approach. There is no room for accusatory anger and arrogance.

5. *Flexible.* Different people have different needs and we must meet their needs by adapting the gospel presentation to different situations.

6. *Sensitive.* Listen and ask questions before you witness. Be sensitive, don't ridicule. Be fair, be patient, be humble.

When we approach cult members for purposes of evangelism, we should view them, not as individuals who embody the full character of evil, but rather as women and men who are reaching toward God.[11] Like Paul, we should affirm their search but not where it has taken them. In Acts 17, Paul intimates that even though the Greeks were very sincere, their sincerity was not enough.

As we seek to present an alternative model of spirituality to cultists—one based on the gospel of Jesus Christ—we must realize the importance of prayer-based evangelism. Only after a commitment to specific and consistent prayer can we ask people entrapped in cults the question, "Have you met Jesus my Lord?"

Finally, be strong in the Lord and in his mighty power. Put on the full armor of God so that you can take your stand against the devil's schemes. For our struggle is not against flesh and blood, but against the rulers, against the authorities, against the powers of this dark world and against the spiritual forces of evil in the heavenly realms. Eph 6:10-12

ONE

Hinduism

Mark Albrecht

HINDUISM—A THUMBNAIL SKETCH

It is often said that Hinduism is the world's oldest religion. Indian writers and scholars in particular have been strong proponents of this theory, giving dates anywhere between 10,000 to 2500 B.C. as a plausible estimate of Hinduism's origins.

However, this is not the case. Modern scholarship has established that the earliest vestiges of the Hindu religion are to be found in the scripture known as the *Rig Veda*, which was probably compiled about 1500 B.C. at the earliest.

This makes Hinduism the world's second oldest religion after Judaism, which was established by God's covenant with Abraham, somewhere between 2000 to 1800 B.C. Thus the Jewish nation and religion was flourishing even during the Egyptian captivity; Moses led the Exodus of the Jews out of Egypt about 1400 B.C.

Hinduism as it is described in the *Rig Veda*, however, bears almost no resemblance to Hinduism today. The religion described in these early scriptures was in fact a garden variety of *polytheism* (belief in many gods) and had many similarities with other Middle Eastern religions of the time.

Modern Hinduism, while it has many diverse expressions, is

founded upon a bedrock of two fundamental philosophical assumptions. The first is the idea that the entire universe is undergirded by an impersonal absolute, a sort of universal spirit, usually called *Brahman*. Hinduism holds that the world is really "Brahman in disguise"—all matter, especially biological and human life, is merely a temporary, illusory manifestation of this universal spirit—not unlike the concept of "the Force" in the movie *Star Wars*.

While modern Hindus frequently use the word "God" to describe Brahman, this is not technically correct, for the word "God" is derived from the Judeo-Christian tradition. In biblical terms, God is an infinite, loving, personal Creator who is *distinct* from his creation. In theological terms, this is called *theism*.

Hinduism, by contrast, generally does not believe in a personal God, nor does it draw a distinction between the Creator and creation. Thus all things, including people, are essentially "God," even if we are unable to perceive this. This is *pantheism*.

The second universally held assumption in Hinduism is the idea of reincarnation. Sometimes called "the transmigration of souls," reincarnation teaches that all forms of life are somehow reborn after death. In the case of humans, this means that individuals are reborn into an improved life situation if they have behaved correctly in their previous life. Conversely, if one has lived a bad life, he or she is reborn as a person who is worse off, experiencing much suffering, affliction, or poverty.

Strangely, these two ideas were absent from early Hinduism, which, as noted earlier, was polytheistic. In the early form, a variety of gods competed for cosmic power and the attention of the human race, not unlike a group of celestial movie stars.

Likewise, reincarnation was nonexistent in the early scriptures. Prior to 1000 B.C. Indian religion held to a form of resurrection in which individuals retained their respective personalities in the afterworld. This is significant in that it shows the gradual philosophic development of Hinduism.

It was not until the *Upanishadic era* (ca. 800 to 500 B.C.) that Hinduism assumed its present form. Nonetheless, Hinduism is the source of all other Asian religions. Buddhism broke off from Hinduism after the life and ministry of Gautama Buddha (ca. 500 B.C.), and other religions, such as India's Jainism and Chinese Taoism, were ultimately derived from Hindu speculations.

Hinduism in the 1990s. Today Hinduism is still chiefly confined to the Indian subcontinent. India itself is about eighty percent Hindu. Nepal, the exotic Himalayan kingdom to the north of India, is the world's only officially Hindu state; King Birendra is revered by his subjects as a Hindu deity.

While there is no one creator God in Hinduism, there are indeed plenty of gods—some estimates put the number as high as thirty million. These lesser deities are all considered to be lower manifestations of the Absolute Brahman, and dwell in a sort of cosmic hierarchy. The two most powerful gods are Shiva and Vishnu. Shiva is sometimes called "the destroyer," while Vishnu is known as "the preserver." Together they are said to balance each other out in an eternal dance of creation, destruction, and re-creation, which is reflected in the doctrine of reincarnation.

Religious Practice. Hindu religious practice revolves around several things. One is a ceremony called the *puja*, which is an act of worship involving the offering of flowers, food, and even animals to specific deities. Meditation on a *mantra* (a sacred word or phrase which is repeated over and over), and *yoga*, which is a combination of meditation and physical austerities and postures, such as the "calisthenics" of hatha yoga taught in many classes in the West, are other facets of Hindu religious practice.

However, the most important feature of modern Hindu practice is the veneration of the *guru*. The guru, sometimes called "swami," is an enlightened master, supposedly a man (always a man, never a woman) who is in his last of many thousands of reincarnations. He is believed to have accumulated an enormous wealth of spiritual power and knowledge as a result of having logged countless years over many lifetimes as he struggled along the spiritual path.

Consequently, the guru is the all-important figure in Hinduism. In comparing Christianity with Hinduism, one might say that the guru occupies about the same status for the devout Hindu as Jesus does to the Christian.

This fact was underscored some years ago when I was traveling through Rishikesh, a most intriguing city on the Ganges River in north India, nestled among the foothills of the Himalayas. A center for both Indian holy men and Hindu pilgrims, Rishikesh is also filled with Western "seekers" who have come to India in search of spiritual truth. After a long conversation on spiritual matters with two Germans sitting next to the river one warm winter day, one of them finally said to me regarding my relationship with Jesus Christ, "Your spiritual master died two thousand years ago. Mine is living in that old monastery up on the hillside. I see him and hear him speak every day."

Hinduism in the West. Hinduism first arrived in the United States and Europe in the latter part of the nineteenth century. The first movement to popularize Hindu ideas in the West was the Theosophical Society, founded in 1875 by Madame Helena Petrovna Blavatsky and Colonel Henry Steel Olcott. Blavatsky and Olcott tirelessly promoted the "esoteric wisdom" of the Orient, while frequently denouncing Christianity as a tired old religion that had outlived its usefulness.

The efforts of the Theosophical Society set the stage for the first genuine Indian guru to arrive in North America. His name was Swami Vivekananda. Vivekananda attended the Parliament of World Religions in Chicago in 1893, where he impressed all the other delegates.

A formidable and dashing figure dressed in red robes, an orange sash, and yellow turban, the swami's excellent command of the English language and powerful message made him an instant celebrity. He was given prominent coverage in the newspapers, which resulted in a nationwide speaking tour that attracted thousands of followers. This led to the establishment of the Vedanta Society in 1894; the society still flourishes throughout North America and Europe, and has been one of the most influential vehicles for the spread of Hindu philosophy outside of India.

After Vivekananda established his influence in the West, others followed. Jiddu Krishnamurti was promoted by the Theosophists as another enlightened master of the age and attracted a large following after World War I.

Paramahansa Yogananda, who arrived in Boston in 1920 and established the Self-Realization Fellowship, was particularly adept at disarming Christians. Yogananda's popular book, *Autobiography of a Yogi* (available in fourteen languages), contains biblical texts which attempt to show that Jesus was a Jewish guru who taught a form of

Hinduism that he had supposedly learned during his travels to India in his early years.

This development was significant because it marked the first systematic attempt to construct a form of *syncretism* (a synthesis or combining of all religions into one) that was to become a central tenet of modern Hinduism and the New Age movement that grew out of it (see p. 30 for a more detailed evaluation of this problem).

After World War II a growing number of Hindu holy men and yoga teachers came to the West, a trend which culminated in the 1960s. The wholesale cultural shift among the youth of the day was accompanied by an intense interest in oriental religions, notably Hinduism and Buddhism. Some of the best known Hindu gurus and groups of that time are the following:

Maharishi Mahesh Yogi and Transcendental Meditation (TM). Perhaps the most visible and certainly the largest of the guru movements, TM has always tried to market itself as a secular, non-religious relaxation technique. The Maharishi, who initiated over one million unwitting people into orthodox Hinduism (a puja of prayers and offerings are dedicated at the altar of Maharishi's dead Hindu master during the initiation ceremony), attained instant celebrity status as the guru of the Beatles and others.

As TM gained in popularity, it was taught in many public high schools across the United States at taxpayer expense. A class action suit was brought against the TM organization in the late 1970s on the grounds that public support for religious indoctrination violated the establishment clause of the first amendment of the United States Constitution, which prohibits state sponsorship of religion. TM lost the case and the Maharishi moved to Switzerland, finally returning to India in 1981. TM still operates a number of centers throughout North America and Europe, but has declined in influence.

The Hare Krishnas/International Society for Krishna Consciousness (ISKCON). Founded by A.C. Bhaktivedanta Prabhupada in 1965, the Hare Krishnas are a well-known Hindu group, chanting on street corners and peddling books in airports. They have declined steadily since Prabhupada's death in 1977, but are still a presence. They worship the Hindu deity Krishna (a form of Vishnu) by chanting his name over one thousand times each day.

The Hare Krishnas represent the Bhakti form of Hinduism, which has some parallels to Christianity in that they regard Krishna as a personal savior of sorts. However, they adhere to the traditional doctrine of reincarnation and rely on the Hindu scripture known as the *Bhagavad Gita*, which speaks of God in traditional pantheistic terms.

The Divine Light Mission (DLM) and Guru Maharaj Ji. The DLM came into prominence in the early 1970s with the advent of Guru Maharaj Ji, the chubby teenage pundit who licked ice cream cones and rode minibikes while giving discourses on Hindu spirituality. Largely a media phenomenon due to his age (fourteen when he first appeared), he nonetheless had a large following of Western disciples.

A power struggle between the guru and his older brother, who also proclaimed himself a guru, led to the gradual dissolution of the DLM. Maharaj Ji now keeps a fairly low profile as a spiritual teacher.

Swami Muktananda. Swami Muktananda, who died in 1982, deserves mention even though he was not as well-known or controversial as the above gurus. The swami, who always wore a knit hat and spoke no English, had about a hundred thousand followers and several hundred centers around the world. He is important because he is more representative of the orthodox line of Hindu gurus in the West.

Muktananda gave frequent discourses on spirituality to seekers and disciples, initiating his followers by touching them with a peacock feather; this technique, called *shaktipat*, usually put the devotee into an immediate trance state, and thereafter the disciple was to become obedient to the guru in all things. This type of obedience and spiritual/psychological dependency on the guru is one of the central elements of Hindu spirituality; gurus are considered incarnations or distilled essences of all that is truly enlightened and divine. Complete subjugation of one's self to the guru is absolutely essential.

Muktananda also popularized an axiom of pantheistic Hindu philosophy by coining the saying, "Worship your own inner self. God dwells within you as you." This cornerstone of Hinduism is a logical extension of pantheism—if "God" is synonymous with the world, then people are also divine—at least at their very core.

Thus *ignorance* of one's innately divine status is the essence of "sin." Consequently, life's goal is to both *realize* and *experience* one's own godly nature. The person who is successful in doing this attains salvation or liberation (*moksha*), and is not reborn into another life of human suffering.

The Vishwa Hindu Parishad (World Hindu Organization). The flood of Hindu teachers to the West in the last three decades has been referred to as the Hindu Countermission to the West. It is a reaction to several centuries of Christian missionary activity (as well as British colonial rule) in India.

The Vishwa Hindu Parishad (VHP) acts as a loose confederation of Hindu groups and lobbyists, with the dual aim of strengthening the Hindu role in India and promoting its spread around the world. As such, it has been the main catalyst and coordinating body for Hindu spiritual masters sent out as missionaries. Although the VHP is not a highly organized conspiracy to destroy Christianity, strategy and networking among influential Hindus is a reality that Christians need to be aware of.

The Hindu Countermission has met with spectacular success in the West. The New Age movement and the shift away from the traditional Judeo-Christian concept of God toward more pantheistic ideas, especially among the under-fifty generation, is a measure of its effectiveness.

One statistic should suffice to illustrate this. At the turn of the century approximately one to two percent of the population of Europe and North America believed in reincarnation. In 1982 the Gallup Poll stated that the figure was about twenty-two percent, varying somewhat from country to country. Most of these people are not formally affiliated with a Hindu or Buddhist teacher, or even a New Age group, but have nonetheless been converted to an essentially Hindu worldview.

PRACTICAL GUIDELINES
FOR EVANGELISM AND APOLOGETICS

There are of course many strategies, tactics, and principles involved in evangelism. Here I will limit myself to three basic principles that I have found helpful.

First, the gospel must be relevant to each person. To put it in the vernacular, one must "scratch where it itches." Each person has primary concerns, values, and a "focus" on life. Determining this *point of contact* is of utmost importance to the evangelist, and is to be done through gently asking, probing, and especially listening. As suggested by the British theologian Michael Green, "One must row his boat slowly around the island of each person's life until he finds that quiet and open bay on which to land." Such an approach also builds up trust, which gives the gospel more credibility and effectiveness.

Second, a good grasp of *apologetics, i.e.*, a reasonable intellectual defense of the faith, is necessary. While God does not call most of us to be scholars or theologians, he does expect us to know *what* we believe and *why* we believe it. In the following pages I will give special attention to apologetics concerning the Hindu worldview.

Third, the gospel is, as St. Paul put it, "the power of God for salvation" (Rom 1:16). The gospel is not a human contrivance that uses psychological ploys and gimmicks, or a commodity to be merchandized like soap. Since the gospel is the message from God and about God, intercessory prayer is also essential, an integral part of effective evangelism.

In dealing with the adherents of Hindu and New Age religious groups, this is especially important, as the devotees have usually undergone a psycho-spiritual bonding experience with the guru or master. These people can become quite fanatical and irrational when confronted with the gospel; therefore, great patience, love, and a prayerful, tactful gospel presentation is necessary. Attacking the guru as a false prophet or degrading his teachings as "unchristian" will only alienate the devotee.

Comparing Religions. In comparing worldviews such as Hinduism and Christianity, it is helpful to have a theological frame of reference by which to evaluate competing belief systems. This enables us to perceive more clearly the differences and similarities on critical points. One such grid compares religions in five major areas of doctrinal concern:

1. *Doctrine of God.* The "God" of Hinduism is basically an impersonal principle which undergirds the universe and emanates the phenomenal world forth out of its own essence. Unfortunately,

such a God is just as flawed as the universe it creates. Thus our imperfect world only mirrors the imperfection of Hinduism's God.

In contrast, the Bible tells us that God is holy and infinite in all respects, yet personal; he is the God who creates things out of nothing by his word of command, and stands apart from and above his creation, loving his creatures with a self-sacrificial love.

2. *Nature of the world.* Hinduism views the world as something which is less than real, an illusory projection of consciousness which is inherently negative, a lamentable by-product of the creative forces of the universe.

The Christian faith, by contrast, sees the world as real, though temporal and fallen. It is part of God's deliberate creation, and as such has a definite purpose and is basically good. The finished creation is portrayed in Genesis (before the Fall) as both real and good.

3. *Human nature.* In Hinduism, people are only transient shells with fleeting personalities that serve to house an "immortal soul" for a lifetime before it moves on into another body in the process of reincarnation. This soul is of course considered a part of God, a spark of the divine fire.

Christianity views people as being made in the image of God (Gen 1:26), and thus humans have both personality and moral responsibility. This personality is not extinguished at death, but is preserved in the resurrection, and does not return to earth in another body. The Bible also teaches that we are not divine, but are creatures made by God. We are also sinful and fallen, in need of forgiveness and a restoration of our broken relationship with God.

4. *Salvation.* In Hinduism, salvation, or liberation from reincarnation, is achieved by strenuous self-effort. The soul must save itself by working off the bonds of *karma* (negative or incorrect actions) accumulated in thousands of incarnations.

The Christian faith insists that eternal life is a free gift from God, and is conferred upon the recipient regardless of merit—or the lack of it. It is only necessary to receive the gift of eternal life and apply it through righteous living.

5. *Evil.* In Hinduism the endless cycle of reincarnation never solves the problem of evil. Evil is an eternal, permanent reality in Hindu philosophy. The idea of evil continuing forever is unthinkable in Christianity. Evil was conquered by the death and

resurrection of Christ and will be put away forever when he returns to judge the world.

All things considered, a fundamental difference between historic orthodox Christianity and the religions of the East lies in their respective focal points. Christianity puts God at the center; he is the object of worship. Hinduism reduces theology to a form of anthropology, making humanity the measure of all things.

Syncretism in the Age of Aquarius. Another issue which frequently arises with regard to Hinduism and Christianity is a form of syncretism, namely, the attempt to make Jesus another Hindu guru.

One of the hallmarks of much of the modern Hindu philosophy promoted by New Age Hindu groups and gurus is the consistent and contrived attempt to reinterpret the life and teaching of Jesus Christ within an esoteric or occult framework. In fact, it would not be excessive to say that some ninety percent of such groups actually go out of their way to give Jesus prominent mention, while downplaying or attacking orthodox Christianity and the church as an antiquated relic that has systematically suppressed Jesus' true teachings for two thousand years.

This approach, which might be called "Hinduized Christianity," is based upon certain assumptions about Christianity which have no basis in historical fact. Principal among them are:

1. Jesus was a normal man who attained enlightenment by mystical asceticism and then became a Jewish guru who wandered about Palestine teaching vague and esoteric mysteries of "Christ consciousness."

2. He was trained by the Jewish Essenes (an apocalyptic group of devoutly religious desert dwellers), as well as other esoteric schools. He went to India and Tibet where he attained enlightenment during his "lost years" between the ages of twelve and thirty.

3. The apostles—especially Paul—perverted Christ's teachings in their writings. His true, secret teachings are to be found in the old Gnostic documents or through contact with "ascended masters" and other spiritual beings.

4. The New Testament as we now have it is a compilation which was edited by a group of bigoted, ignorant, and narrow-minded elderly churchmen who did a quick cut-and-paste job on the Bible sometime after the fourth century.

5. The church was forced to convene several ecumenical councils (Nicaea and Constantinople are usually named) in order to suppress Gnostic and pantheistic doctrines and to expel such teachings as reincarnation.

6. True Christianity is based upon a realization that the universe is divine and that people need to achieve enlightenment (not salvation) by realizing and experiencing their true and essential divinity.

Before dealing with these issues, some general comments on this problem are in order. First, the genuineness of Christianity—or any other religion—must be discerned by sound scholarship and historical bases, as well as textual and scriptural authenticity.

For example, it is impossible to understand the New Testament apart from its theological, cultural, and historical background in Judaism. The Old Testament and the Jewish tradition were rigidly monotheistic, upheld a radical Creator-creation distinction, and did not practice any sort of pantheistic mysticism. Hindu ideas and practices, such as polytheism and occult rites, cannot be reconciled with the Old Testament's theology.

To understand the life and teaching of Jesus, this Jewish background must be kept in mind, especially when reading the four Gospels. Also, the very well-documented history of the early church, the process of apostolic succession, and the development of the New Testament canon must all be correctly understood if one is to determine what true Christianity is.

Furthermore, later refinements such as the formation of the creeds and the development of Christian theology—also well documented—cannot be summarily dismissed as the work of a few cranks. The evidence in support of Christian orthodoxy is so entrenched and overwhelming that it takes a deliberate attempt to ignore and twist the facts in order to refute it.

Second, such a refutation is not really a refutation. It is simply an emotional argument masquerading behind fabricated evidence. Herein lies the real tragedy: many people believe such lies and half-truths because they have forgotten how to *think critically*. The phenomenon of Hinduized Christianity plays upon the theological and logical naivete, and intellectual laziness of many of the spiritual seekers of our day.

People allow the "spiritual teacher" to do their thinking for them. The teacher or guru says, "Just listen: I'll tell you how it is. I have the essence of cosmic truth and a deeper understanding of Christ's true teachings, so just pay attention to me. Never mind reading the Bible or church history or Christian theology. Just listen to my explanation."

The Hinduized Christianity of the modern era which is promoted by the New Age gurus and groups is based on intellectual mistakes and erroneous scholarship, not to mention an intentional twisting of the facts. The uncritical acceptance of such evidence is the greatest weakness of the contemporary syncretist movement.

A summary apologetic of the six points of Hinduized Christianity follows:

1. *Jesus was a Jewish guru.* Jesus was, in fact, a radical monotheist who taught that salvation (not enlightenment) was attained through repentance and the forgiveness of sin. The word "consciousness" is not found anywhere in the Bible, and any attempt to say that Jesus taught "Christ consciousness" is unsupportable by the Scripture.

2. *Jesus spent his lost years in the mystery schools of the Orient.* The fact is that no one knows where Jesus spent his lost years between ages of twelve and thirty, which are not mentioned in the Gospels. That is precisely why they are called lost. A reading of the Gospels shows that even if he did go to the Orient, he never returned to teach anything resembling the esoteric doctrines of Hindu and Buddhist pantheism. Apart from that, there is no historical evidence to suggest that Jesus traveled outside of Palestine. The so-called "grave of Jesus" in north India dates to the eighteenth century and can be traced to an old rumor aimed at discrediting British rule in India. The Essenes were orthodox Jews who did not engage in pantheistic speculations.

3. *The apostles perverted Jesus' teachings.* On the contrary, great care was taken in the early church to make sure that the apostles were not teaching a "different gospel" from the one the original disciples received. Paul relates that he was grilled at some length by the rest of the apostles as to the content of his teaching, since he had not been with Jesus during his earthly ministry (*cf.* Gal 2:2).

4. *The New Testament was edited after the fourth century.* The New Testament was complete by the end of the first century and had assumed its present form by A.D. 197, according to the list of St. Irenaeus. Although it was not officially canonized until 397 at the Council of Carthage under Augustine, textual scholars have shown that it was not tampered with in any substantial way. The Gnostic Gospels of the second and third centuries were rejected by consensus. They were not written by eyewitnesses, being of a late date (the four Gospels were all written in the first century by eyewitness account), they were of dubious authorship, and they did not conform to apostolic teaching.

5. *Special councils were convened to condemn pantheistic teachings.* The early ecumenical councils were called to deal with Christology, matters of ecclesiology, and theological interpretation. Even the persistent and nettlesome Gnostic heresy did not require a special council to refute it; this was ably handled by the early church's apologists, such as Irenaeus. Reincarnation was at best a marginal issue in the early church, mentioned only in passing by such church fathers as Justin Martyr, Jerome, and Origen.

6. *True Christianity is based on the pantheistic notion of a "Divine Within."* This basic tenet of Hindu philosophy is simply not found in the Old or New Testament and has always been rejected by the Judeo-Christian tradition. Although many Hindus like to cite Luke 17:21—"The Kingdom of God is within you"—this is an inadequate translation of the Greek and is found only in the old King James Version. Hindu concepts such as existential enlightenment, yoga, and reincarnation are utterly alien to biblical Christianity.

Nearly all of the esoteric New Age and Hindu groups feel compelled to explain away the life of Christ and Christianity in this way, although such systematic and contrived attempts to reinterpret Christianity are not utilized by the same groups in regard to other religions and teachers, such as Buddha, Krishna, Muhammad, or Confucius. The unparalleled influence of Jesus and the gospel through the centuries and around the world has been too great to be ignored.

Perhaps, lurking at the bottom of all such speculation about Jesus is the fear that he really is what orthodox Christianity claims: the unique incarnation of the transcendent, living God, who conquered sin, suffering, and death by his own sacrificial death—the living foe of all spiritual error.

The twentieth-century church needs to develop a concise and consistent refutation of Hinduized Christianity, for it is becoming a major theological challenge of our time.

FINAL THOUGHTS

Having said all this, a brief examination of some of the major problems associated with Hindu pantheism should be considered.

1. The existence of evil and suffering is never resolved. Since the absolute or "God" of Hinduism creates both bad and good in eternal cycles of creation and dissolution, the current status quo is unending, constituting an eternal cycle of chaos, aimless wandering, injustice, and repression. Furthermore, the Creation and the Fall are *synonymous and simultaneous,* as the first primordial creative emanation from the absolute contains evil, suffering, and deceit, as manifested in our world. Thus the foulest deeds and thoughts of humanity literally become attributes of God.

Moreover, reincarnation certainly does not solve this problem, but instead pushes evil further out of reach, procrastinating moral responsibility and perpetuating suffering in life after life. Thus "bad karma" multiplies exponentially, and it is difficult to see how this sorry syndrome can ever be reversed.

2. There is not an adequate basis for knowledge (epistemology) in Hinduism. The creative act is by definition one of illusion and deceit. This is a fundamental tenet of the Hindu worldview. The world is called *maya* (illusion) in Hinduism, and all life forms are trapped in *avidya* (ignorance) as a result of this lamentable creative default. Therefore, the inherently deceptive nature of the Absolute, which always manifests itself in disguise, is ultimately untrustworthy, especially in such important matters as faith and salvation.

3. Life is essentially meaningless in the context of Hindu philosophy. On an individual level, there is only eventual annihilation, even for the guru. Salvation or liberation in Hinduism is often illustrated by comparing the enlightened soul to a drop of water that falls into the ocean, to be forever dissolved in the impersonal absolute. Such a notion is essentially no different from the atheist's conception of death.

This despairing notion, coupled with the idea of reincarnation— where each individual personality is dissolved at death to be reborn as "someone else" who cannot recall his previous life—leads one to conclude that there is very little worth for the individual personality. The same can be said for the universe as a whole. Hinduism's greatest philosopher, Shankaracharya, stated that the only purpose of Brahman's creation of the world was *lila*, which may be translated as "sport"—in other words, a game for Brahman's amusement. (See J.A.B. van Buitenen, *Ramajuna on the Bhagavad Gita* [Delhi: Motilal Banarsidass, 1969] p. 69.) If this is the case, resignation and nihilism would seem to be the most logical response to Hinduism.

4. The confusion of God with one's own inner being, often expressed in the phrase "All is One," is really a refined form of blasphemy, at least from the Christian perspective.

A FINAL WORD

This chapter has advanced a *polemic* (a philosophical attack or argument) against the teachings of Hinduism. It is written for a Christian audience. When evangelizing Hindus, however, it would be most unwise to attack them as being "wrong," thereby setting yourself up as "right." Such an approach only serves to put people on the defensive, which very rarely results in a conversion! Therefore, I do not recommend giving all or any of this chapter to Hindus or Westerners who sympathize with Hindu beliefs to read.

Rather, it is intended to give Christians a background in both Hindu beliefs and a Christian apologetic that you must adapt to the individual situation.

Never think of evangelism as "winning the argument." Gentle persuasion and an attitude of Christian love and concern must be paramount. Listen and ask questions before you present the gospel. Be sensitive. Narrow-minded intolerance and accusatory anger will only discredit the truth of the Christian message.

> If I speak in the tongues of men and of angels, but have not love, I am only a noisy gong, or a clanging cymbal. If I have the gift of prophecy, and can fathom all mysteries and all knowledge, and if I have a faith that can move mountains, but have not love, I am nothing. If I give away all my possessions to the poor and surrender my body to the flames, but have not love, I gain nothing.
>
> Love is patient, love is kind. It does not envy, it does not boast, it is not proud. It is not rude, it is not self-seeking, it is not easily angered, it keeps no record of wrongs. Love does not delight in evil but rejoices in the truth. It always protects, always trusts, always hopes, always perseveres. 1 Cor 13:1-7

Love also conquers all things—especially in evangelism.

TWO

Buddhism

J. Isamu Yamamoto

I T USED TO BE that we could readily spot people of another faith on a typical North American street by the way they dressed and by the way they acted. Or at least that was what we might have thought—though our assumptions were actually awry. Now it is obvious that there are a multitude of people in our society who profess beliefs other than Judaism or Christianity—not the least of whom are Buddhists. And their appearance and behavior are not unlike the appearance and behavior of any other North American.

WHO ARE THEY?

Buddhism is currently making rapid strides in becoming an organized religion in the United States. In 1988 the World Fellowship of Buddhists, which represents all the schools of Buddhism throughout the world, assembled for the first time in the United States, specifically in Los Angeles, where a vast population of Buddhists resides. Buddhist leaders at that conference declared that Buddhism had evolved as a major religion in the United States. They also estimated that over one thousand Buddhist organizations and perhaps as many as four million Buddhists are in the United States.

Faced with these imposing figures, we must ask: Are the Buddhists in our society Asians, Anglos, or both? Are they neighbors and people we work with? Do we go to school with them? Could they even be in our families? In fact, a Buddhist could fit any of these descriptions. And for that reason, it is imperative for us to know what they believe if we wish to share the gospel with them.

What they believe, however, may be very different from one Buddhist to another. Not only are there scores of Buddhist schools whose cultural and historical backgrounds can be quite diverse, but the level of religious commitment of Buddhists also varies. For example, most of my Buddhist relatives on my father's side are extremely religious; while on my mother's side, those who are Buddhists are so in name only.

Few of my devout Buddhist relatives possess a comprehensive, penetrating understanding of Buddhist doctrines. They are practicing Buddhists because that is their cultural identity. They are like many people who identify themselves as Christians—who attend services regularly, tithe regularly, pray at the appropriate times, who reserve an important place for religion in their lives and uphold a high ethical code, but who would never allow God to impose himself in the totality of their lives.

Buddhists of this religious orientation must not merely break a habit, but they must change their identity if they are to become Christians. You could know Buddhist doctrines better than they do, but that knowledge will play at best a minor role in your evangelism. I have had many interesting discussions with them, but that is all they were—two people sharing their worldviews. As one aunt said to me, "With all its flaws and weaknesses, I am still a Buddhist and will always be a Buddhist." Argument will never win this person over.

The most successful evangelism that I have seen with these people is "involvement." When they can see the teachings of Christ at work in our marriages, in how we deal with our children, in our behavior at work, and in our treatment of them, then they take notice of who we are, inquire about our ethics, and quietly process the little things that we say about our Savior. But, of course, they can never see these things unless we intertwine our lives with theirs.

My other relatives are a different story. They do not have an ethical system that keeps their lives in balance. Their lives seem to be more of a roller-coaster ride with fleeting thrills and constant uncertainties. They are like many North Americans who attend church now and then—usually only at weddings and funerals, who list themselves as part of this or that religious group, but who are either indifferent or hostile to religion.

Buddhists often have a perception of Christianity that is loaded with misconceptions. What they know of Christians is determined by movies, television, and popular books—and we know that those media often regard Christians as narrow-minded hypocrites. It is no wonder with all the modern-day Elmer Gantrys making the headlines in the tabloids.

Whenever you share your faith with someone, you always have to sweep away silly notions and justified prejudices; but with these Buddhists the broom must be of sturdier stock. Of course, your life must reflect the teachings of Christ, but you must also clearly present the gospel, firmly refuting every erroneous caricature of yourself and what you believe. Once all the clutter is cleared from their minds, they will listen with interest about the love Jesus has for them. As a matter of fact, I have seen more Buddhists in this group come to Christ than any other group.

My relatives represent two kinds of people who are inclined toward Buddhism because of their cultural background. In my experiences, I have discovered that most Asians fit in one or the other category if they are not Christians. But there is still one other significant group of Buddhists. They are people of African or European descent who have embraced Buddhism. And their bonding to Buddhism is very different.

Most of these Buddhists may not understand all the fine points of Buddhist doctrines, but they can articulate the fundamental principles of the particular school of Buddhism in which they are involved. Many were raised in Judaism or Christianity, but they have renounced their former religious identity and have committed themselves to the teachings of the Buddha. Some even have a clear understanding of the Christian faith, but they believe the way of Buddha is the truth.

Of the three groups of Buddhists, an understanding of Buddhism is most necessary in dialoguing with Western Buddhist converts. These people are attracted to the ethical moderation in most

Buddhist schools; they are fascinated by Buddhism's apparent toleration that other religions seem to lack; but most of all they are enamored by the supreme compassion of the Buddha. Thus, we need to know who the Buddha was, what he taught, and why he is revered by so many people today—even in this country.

WHO WAS THIS MAN AND WHAT DID HE SEEK?

The biography of Siddhartha Gautama was not written during his lifetime. The earliest available accounts of his life were collected some three hundred years after his death. Since then, both historical and legendary descriptions of his life have been included in the Pali Canon and in Sanskrit accounts. Historians have debated where to draw the line between history and legend, but whether the stories of Gautama the Buddha be true or myth, his life has been and still is an inspiration and model for all Buddhists.

Nevertheless, I find it interesting that Western Buddhist converts especially will attack the historicity of Jesus Christ and the authenticity of the Bible, and yet they will accept uncritically the traditional biography and teachings of the Buddha. A Christian who is sharing his or her faith with a Buddhist would do well to know why Judeo-Christian texts are much more reliable than both Buddhist *and* Hindu texts.

Siddhartha Gautama was probably born in 563 B.C. and died about eighty years later. His father was King Suddhodana Gautama, a chieftain of the Sakya clan in ancient Bharata, a small region on the Indian slope of the Himalayas in the borderland between India and Nepal.

During his infancy, Siddhartha Gautama was visited by a sage, Asita, who prophesied that Siddhartha would either become a great ruler like his father if he dwelt in his father's house, or he would become a Buddha, a remover of ignorance from the world, if he went forth into the world. King Suddhodana knew that the sight of human misery would cause his son to leave home and seek for truth. Since the king wanted his son to follow his footsteps to the throne, he issued strict orders to his subjects that the young prince was not to see any evil or suffering.

Despite the diligence of his father to sequester him from evil and suffering, as a young adult Siddhartha eluded the royal attendants and drove his chariot through the city. He saw an old man, a leper, a corpse, and an ascetic. He realized then that life was full of sorrows and that happiness was an illusion. He became aware of human suffering.

Siddhartha left his family and kingdom on the same night during which his wife, Yashodara, gave birth to his son, Rahula. The decision to leave was painful for him, but now that his son could continue the royal line, he could commence his spiritual quest for truth. Thus, he began a pilgrimage of inquiry and asceticism.

For six or seven years Siddhartha sought communion with the supreme cosmic spirit, first through the teachings of two Brahman hermits and then in the company of five monks. He practiced the traditional methods of asceticism such as fasting. Other physical austerities included sleeping on brambles to mortify the desires of his body and abstaining from sitting by crouching on his heels to develop his concentration.

Despite all these efforts, he did not succeed in attaining truth. Finally, he realized that his life as an ascetic was of no greater value than his previous life as a prince. Self-torture was vain and fruitless; privation was no better than pleasure. He understood, then, the importance of the Middle Way.

The doctrine of the Middle Way must be underlined because it is a philosophical principle that both appeals to many Westerners and is an ethical touchstone of many Asian Buddhists. You can see it in the wisdom and serenity of Miyagi of *The Karate Kid* and Splinter of *The Teenage Mutant Ninja Turtles*, both extremely popular today.

On the wide bank of Meranjana at Gaya near the village of Uruvella, Siddhartha sat at the foot of a fig tree. There he experienced the revelation of liberating awareness, the way that provides escape from the cruel bondage of reincarnation. He discovered the Four Noble Truths, and henceforth he was the Buddha, the Enlightened One.

These four truths include:

1. *Life is full of sorrow.* Every person is born, becomes old, and dies. Suffering marks an endless cycle of lives. Therefore, reincarnation is a curse.

2. *The origin of suffering is ignorance.* People are ignorant of who they are and what life is. From ignorance proceeds desire for immaterial

and material things. There is neither eternal youth, nor ultimate power, nor absolute joy. All suffer because of ignorance.

3. *A person can break this cycle of rebirths by realizing that the essence of all things, including the soul, is emptiness.* This differs from the Hindu understanding of the soul. In Hinduism, union is sought between the Universal Soul (*Brahman*) and the individual soul (*Atman*) to bring about a oneness just as a raindrop becomes one with the ocean. In Buddhism, there is no soul. Rather, a consciousness is reborn and needs to be "extinguished" just as a candle flame is blown out. This consciousness is not a soul (as the Hindu or Christian would describe a soul), but it is the causal result of ignorance, and it is extinguished when one realizes the emptiness of its existence.

Christians who have written on Buddhism in the past have particularly misunderstood the Buddhist doctrine of emptiness. They have denounced and ridiculed this concept as being nihilistic, inferring that only a fool would believe in the Void. The belief in emptiness is not the belief in nothing or the belief that nothing matters. Rather, it is an inexplicable acceptance of ultimate reality as it is without qualifications. In fact, when you seriously consider the real sufferings of humanity, then this resolution does not seem so absurd.

4. *The path that leads to the cessation of suffering has eight steps:* right views, right aspirations, right speech, right conduct, right mode of living (that is, free from luxury), right effort, right awareness, and right concentration. By walking the eightfold path, a person will eventually (after many successive reincarnations) receive enlightenment. Although the Buddhist doctrine of extinction may seem nihilistic to Christians, living a pure life to end a cycle of lives full of suffering is understood to be idealistic rather than fatalistic.

After his Enlightenment, the Buddha was faced with a crucial decision. He could either renounce the world and withdraw with his knowledge, or he could remain with people and share the Four Noble Truths with those who sought deliverance from reincarnation. Out of his compassion for others, he chose the latter.

This act of self-sacrifice must also be underlined because it is the great theme of the Buddha's life and teachings. It is what binds the heart of the Buddhist believer to the Buddha. Unlike Jesus who ministered to people for three years and suffered a humiliating death on the cross, the Buddha served others for forty-five years and passed away peacefully. When you share with a Buddhist, inevitably you will have to deal with these two contrasting images.

THE MANY FACES OF AMERICAN BUDDHISM

As the various forms of Buddhism have arrived in the United States, there has been a general desire among these schools to achieve some type of unity. Buddhist schools, however, respond to and interpret the teachings of the Buddha quite differently, in part, because a systematic Buddhist theology apparently was not put in written form until four centuries after the Buddha's death. Consequently schisms occurred within the Buddhist community during those centuries over the content of the Buddha's teachings, and two major philosophies emerged within Buddhism: *Theravada* and *Mahayana* Buddhism.

Theravada Buddhism contains major points of doctrine that differ from the beliefs of many Mahayana schools. Most significantly, the Theravadins revere the Buddha as a great ethical teacher, but not as a god as many of the Mahayanists do. Furthermore, their teachings are reserved for the *Arhat* (a saint who has accomplished the Four Noble Truths in Theravada Buddhism) and not for the common people, another departure from many of the Mahayana schools that exalt the *Bodhisattva* (a being who seeks Enlightenment but delays Buddhahood in order first to save others with his own merits).

Yana means "vehicle" or "the way of progress." Thus, through *yana* the Buddhist crosses the river of rebirth and arrives upon the shore of *nirvana*. The *Arhat* is one who has achieved his or her own deliverance from reincarnation or who has crossed the river of rebirth alone; the *Bodhisattva* is one who seeks liberation from suffering for all creatures and conveys many to the shore of nirvana. Nirvana has different meanings: to one Buddhist, it could mean being extinguished; to another, it could mean heaven—a temporary state of bliss before ultimately being extinguished.

It is especially important to understand the figure and role of the *Bodhisattva* because to many Buddhists the *Bodhisattva* is like a Christ-figure who bears the sins of others so that they can reach paradise. Often when you share Jesus with them, they will respond by saying, "Why do we need Christ, we have our *Bodhisattva* [whoever that might be]?" Like many other questions previously asked, this question will be answered shortly.

Representatives of the Theravada philosophy in the West are primarily from Southeast Asia. During and since the Vietnam War, many immigrants from this area have relocated in North America, bringing with them their culture and their fundamentalist branch of Buddhism. Other advocates of Theravada Buddhism are Westerners such as Henry S. Olcott, who with Madame Blavatsky organized the Theosophical Society, of which many North Americans are active members.

Some Buddhist schools in the Mahayana branch of Buddhism have shifted the focus away from the doctrine of emptiness over the centuries. Instead, they concentrate on a Western paradise, a place of bliss where faithful Buddhists reside until they achieve ultimate "extinction." It is not that the doctrine of emptiness is removed from their philosophy, but rather that extinction is delayed in their spiritual odyssey in favor of a place which those Buddhists regard with solace and hope—that is, a Western paradise.

Many Japanese-American Buddhists believe in Amida Buddha and follow the teachings of Shinran Shonin (1173-1262), the founder of *Jodo-Shinshu*, which fosters the belief in a Western paradise. Although many important Buddhist schools, such as Zen and Tibetan Buddhism, dismiss the Amidist doctrines, many Asians believe that faith in Amida Buddha's compassion will secure them a place in paradise. Unlike many of his predecessors, Shinran preached to the masses and held that only by faith can a believer be saved. Whoever surrenders to the Buddha and accepts him as savior would receive admission into paradise.

Asian Buddhists of the Amida schools have also westernized their religion in North America. Buddhists in Asia might visit a temple or shrine any day of the week, but in the West they assemble on Sundays, conduct Sunday schools, and call their places of worship churches. Moreover, the architecture of their churches is similar to many unassuming Protestant buildings.

A few years ago I heard a Buddhist priest speak at my uncle's funeral. He told us not to grieve for Uncle Ben because he was a faithful believer who is in heaven with Buddha. He went on to say we will not enter heaven by our works but by having faith in the almighty compassion of Amida Buddha. As I listened to him, I thought how easy it would be to switch Jesus' name for the Buddha's.

Zen and Tibetan Buddhism not only retain the cultural features of Japan and Tibet but also emphasize spiritual techniques over a simple faith. Westerners who have rejected what they regard as Christian doctrines and culture gravitate toward the meditation schools of Buddhists because of those distinctions. They do not want a savior. They want to attain their spiritual goals through their own efforts.

The writings of D.T. Suzuki are chiefly responsible for the popularity of Zen in the West. In theory and practice, Zen meditation has been particularly attractive to spiritual seekers who are keen to promote a renewal of mystical contemplation. They are intrigued by Zen *Koans* (meditation statements that cannot be resolved or understood by the intellect and thus cut through the rational process of the mind to attain enlightenment) in order to achieve *satori* (the experiential realization that all is one and that duality is the illusion of the mind).

Zen Buddhists seek truth through meditation, and *Zazen* (*za* means sitting and *zen* means meditation) can only be performed through self-effort. The Zen Buddhist must have faith in his or her own Buddha-nature. To have faith in the Buddha is irrelevant. A person does not practice Zen to become a Buddha; a person practices Zen because he or she is a Buddha.

Tibetan Buddhism is most noted for its tantric teachings, a mystical belief system that incorporates magical procedures in the attainment of supernatural powers. Known as the Short Path, the seeker employs occultic techniques to reach enlightenment much more quickly and through far fewer lifetimes than would otherwise be necessary through other Buddhist practices.

Another significant doctrine that the Tibetan Buddhists absorb is *Skaktism*, a Hindu belief system that worships the divine power of the consort of a particular god. They regard the union of male and female as the spiritual symbol for achieving nirvana. Those Tibetan Buddhists, or tantric Buddhists in the West, who are engaged in Skaktism believe that sexual union between a man and woman during sacred rituals will accelerate the attainment of Perfection.

One more notable Buddhist movement in the West is *Nichiren*

Shoshu Buddhism, known in Japan as *Soka Gakkai*. This school of Buddhism was founded by Nichiren (1222-82), who denounced other Buddhist teachers as heretics. Nichiren taught that the efficacy of chanting *Namu-myoho-renge-kyo* ("reverence to the Wonderful Law of the Lotus") coupled with a zealous life dedicated to the principles of the Buddha result in salvation.

The Nichiren Shoshu also emphasizes closeness among its members. Discussion groups are a high priority along with the stress on family conversions. This close unity is a major reason why this group has grown so remarkably since the 1960s. Members of the Nichiren Shoshu worship at a small altar and chant an invocation in order to fulfill their desires and thereby experience happiness. They are quick to note the *Namu-myoho-renge-kyo* is the essence of all life. Therefore, the true goal of their meditation is to become one with the cosmic universe, thus allowing the object of their desires to flow naturally to themselves.

WHICH IMAGE?

So far many questions have been asked and few answers have been given. In my own spiritual quest for truth I have had to answer these questions for myself. But more importantly I have had to determine which questions were the most relevant in contrasting Buddhism with Christianity.

You might strike up a conversation with a cultural Buddhist, a nominal Buddhist, or a Buddhist convert. You will naturally interact differently with that person, depending on that person's personality, circumstances, and commitment to his or her religion. Whatever the case, understanding the contrast between Buddhist and Christian teaching in the following areas could be decisive in the conversion of your Buddhist friend:

1. Buddhist teaching denies the existence of the soul. By contrast the Bible teaches that men and women have souls. Their lives must be defined in terms of their creation by God, their dependence on God, and their relationship to God. Death does not destroy their souls, as Jesus indicates (Mt 10:28).

One member of my family who is a nominal Buddhist tells me

that when he dies, he will enter the grave and that will be it for him. Another relative, who is a devout Buddhist, tells me that he hopes to end his cycle of rebirths and join Buddha in heaven. Whether it is becoming dust in the wind or residing temporarily in a spiritual haven, the long and short of it is that there is finality.

Jesus, on the other hand, tells us that he has reserved a place for us in heaven (Jn 14:3-4), not a temporary resting place before we are extinguished, but a new Jerusalem where we retain our identities eternally in personal communion with a loving God and Savior (Rv 21).

2. The New Testament denies the doctrine of reincarnation. People die only *once* and are judged on the basis of one life (Heb 9:27). The Christian's hope is not the breaking of a cycle of rebirths, but to have eternal life in Christ (1 Thes 5:9-10).

Too many people in the West view reincarnation as a delightful possibility. To think you might have been Napoleon or Marie Antoinette or even Jesus Christ might be amusing, but it ignores the seriousness with which Asians regard reincarnation—that it is a *curse*.

3. In biblical teaching, the origin of suffering is not one's ignorance, but one's sinfulness. While Scripture warns against relating all individual suffering to individual sin, it does base the existence of suffering in the world in the Fall. By contrast with Buddhist teaching, the gospel summons disciples to share in Christ's sufferings (Rom 8:16-17), not to be detached from all suffering.

The Western church has spawned self-help workshops, seminars on self-improvement and success, and a focus on happiness and wealth, which confuse the message of the gospel to many Asians who see little difference between the affluence of the Western church and their own detachment from suffering. If Christians want to share the good news of Jesus Christ, they must enter into what he did, not into suffering for the sake of suffering, but into suffering for the sake of righteousness and truth, and for the sake of others. Jesus stood up for the oppressed, for the social outcasts, and was consequently rejected himself. What Jesus did—dying on the cross, suffering for others—is unique, but Christian materialism and self-centeredness often mask his uniqueness.

When Jesus Christ is shared with Buddhists, his sacrifice as well as his resurrection must be emphasized and contrasted with the Buddhist teachings on detachment and emptiness. Buddhists must see that Christians are willing to suffer for others, just as Jesus suffered for others. Such a testimony to cultural and Western Buddhists would be unique and powerful.

North Americans are being exposed to Buddhism and Christianity. They have two ways before them in which to deal with suffering: the way of the Buddha and the way of Christ. Bishop Stephen Neill portrays this contrast well in *Christian Faith and Other Religions* (p. 123-24):

Why suffer? That is the ultimate question. It comes to sharp and challenging expression in the contrast between the serene and passionless Buddha and the tortured figure on the Cross. In Jesus we see One who looked at suffering with eyes as clear and calm as those of the Buddha. He saw no reason to reject it, to refuse it, to eliminate it. He took it into himself and felt the fullness of its bitterness and horror; by the grace of God he tasted death for every man. But he does not believe that suffering is wholly evil; by the power of God it can be transformed into a redemptive miracle. Suffering is not an obstacle to deliverance, it can become part of deliverance itself. And what he was he bids his children be—the world's sufferers, in order that through suffering the world may be brought back to God.

The Buddhist ideal is that of passionless benevolence. The Christian ideal is that of compassion. When argument has done its best, we must perhaps leave the two ideals face to face. We can only ask our Buddhist friend to look long and earnestly on the Cross of Christ, and to ask himself whether, beyond the peace of the Buddha, there may not be another dimension of peace to the attainment of which there is no way other than the Way of the Cross.

Many people believe that all religions are essentially the same. Different religions may guide people along different paths, but they all lead ultimately to the same goal. But is that assumption true, especially for Buddhists and Christians? Does the way of serenity in the Buddha and the way of suffering in Christ lead to the same summit? The answer is no. The Buddha taught that life is full of sorrow that will continue through countless lifetimes unless we are finally delivered by being extinguished. Jesus promised eternal life with God and his people for those who place their trust in him. The teachings of the Buddha and Jesus Christ cannot both be true. Either there is life beyond the grave or there is nothingness.

The Bible speaks of a God beyond human wisdom. The Bible speaks of a God who created us, who cared for us, who delivered us; a God beyond the furthest reaches of human thought and experience. But he remains a God who embraces those who seek him and gives them his thoughts and his experiences. The Bible speaks of a God beyond who answers all questions, who satisfies all yearnings, who fulfills all needs. The God beyond is present in the person of Jesus.

Those who have given themselves to Jesus Christ have the assurance that beyond the grave suffering shall be at an end and that they shall live with God forever. We know our God and are satisfied, but until the grave we still live in a world of suffering.

The Buddha certainly taught a high ethical morality. The Amida Buddha certainly is a symbol of compassion and mercy. But beyond the Buddha is emptiness, and extinction does not answer the needs of humanity. In Christ, however, is a life of joy and peace throughout eternity, for he said, "Surely I will be with you always, to the very end of the age."

THREE

The New Age

Gordon Lewis

P ERSONAL AND WORLD PROBLEMS have taken on such cosmic pro-
portions that the editors of *The New Age Journal* seek a "new
spirituality."[1] Dissatisfied with inadequate secular educational
philosophies and irrelevant Christianity, New Age leaders are
looking for spiritual experiences that will enable them to get the
most out of every moment of life, preserve the eco-system, and
inaugurate world peace.

THE CHALLENGE OF NEW AGE NETWORKING

Determined to transform individuals throughout the whole
world to their spirituality, New Agers present a major challenge to
Christians at the end of the twentieth century and the beginning of
the twenty-first. Since the Beatles sought out Maharishi Mahesh
Yogi, countless celebrities have been reached in all segments of
society—entertainment, media, psychology, medicine, science, social work, and education. New Age leaders spearheaded a major
cultural shift in the Western world. Virtually uninfluential concepts
in the 1950s have become household words in the 1990s—karma,
reincarnation, enlightenment, meditation.

Why have the New Agers' missions to the West achieved such remarkable success? Doubtless many reasons could be given, but I mention three as a challenge to Christian witnesses.

1. New Age networking has been successful in the information age because of *faithfulness to its "great commission" to transform individuals through outreach*. The following quote has been attributed to Robert Muller, retired United Nations Assistant Secretary-General:

Decide to network
Use every letter you write
Every conversation you have
Every meeting you attend
To express your fundamental beliefs and dreams
Affirm to others the vision of the world you want
   Network through thought
   Network through action
   Network through spirit
You are the center of the world
You are a free immensely powerful source of life and goodness
   Affirm it
   Spread it
   Radiate it
Think night and day about it
And you will see a miracle happen:
the greatness of your own life.
In a world of big powers, media, and monopolies
But of five billion individuals
Networking is the new freedom
   the new democracy
a new form of happiness.

Unless Christians make the most of evangelistic possibilities in this information age, we may be overwhelmed by the response to New Age infiltration in every aspect of society.

2. The success of New Age networking must be traced to *a dynamic spirituality applied to everyday life*. While Christians offer boring, seemingly irrelevant doctrines of sanctification, New Age evangelists have won many to what seems to be a spirituality that makes a difference in the world. An influential work by the editors of *The*

New Age Journal is *Chop Wood, Carry Water: A Guide to Finding Spiritual Fulfillment in Everyday Life.* It is a guide for all those who want to live everyday life as part of the spiritual path.[2] In several best-selling books, Shirley MacLaine, New Age networker par excellence, exhibits the relevance of her New Age ideas to her life.

In response to works like these, Christian witnesses need to exhibit the resources of the abundant life provided by Christ and enabled by the Holy Spirit to overcome financial concerns, marital concerns, child-rearing problems, careers going nowhere, addiction to drugs and alcohol, fears, anxiety, and depression. Christians not coping with everyday pressures in life are not likely to convince New Agers that Christianity is a better way. Effective Christian witnesses to New Age people will demonstrate the superior quality of a spirituality influenced by the Holy Spirit rather than other alleged spirits.

3. New Age networking appeals because it *presents a creative world vision.* Observes Paul McGuire in *Evangelizing the New Age,*

All across the world, major conferences and symposiums are being held that will shape the future of our planet and many are devoid of Christian leaders. Such conferences will deal with topics like tangible solutions for our common future, networking global consciousness, global issues which require immediate attention, and a whole spiritual-political agenda that will co-ordinate the human potential movement, the scientific community, political groups, diplomats, environmental experts, and activists.

In the scientific and media fields, global New Age conferences are being organized that will transform the worlds of medical technology, hospitals, psychiatry, nutrition, and education. Once again we see Christians absent from the debate.[3]

To appeal to New Agers we need to develop a relevant Christian spirituality that fits into an even more attractive worldview and future vision. "The basic problem of Christians in this country [United States] in the last eighty years or so," said Francis Schaeffer, "in regard to society and in regard to government, is that they have seen things in bits and pieces instead of totals."[4] We need to prepare to present a case for a Christian theistic worldview, belief system, and scale of values.

Unless Evangelical Christians are as committed to using every means available both to convert individuals to a life beyond materialism and to create a new vision for the world, we are in for many tragic surprises. If Christians wait until fifty-one percent of the citizens of our country think all is one and that there is no ultimate difference between God and humans, good and evil, truth and error, animals and humans, Christians may find their freedoms severely limited. It seems that according to the New Age perspective one is free to create any reality he wants, except orthodox Christianity. While there is still the freedom to do so, every Christian leader, parent, teacher, and lay person needs to be concerned about witnessing to New Agers.

DISTINCTIVE PROBLEMS OF EVANGELIZING NEW AGERS

How do you witness to people who have been personally transformed by some New Age practice? Do you compare emotional decibels in the testimonies? How do you reach those who think they are God already? Why worry about sin, when it is just wrong thinking or illusory thought? Why turn to Jesus when there are present day gurus who can show us the way to experience God? Why study the Bible when you can have a hotline to heaven? Why should they think your view is closer to the truth? They are doing something for world peace, are you?

Bumper sticker answers will not suffice! We are dealing with people committed in different degrees to different ultimate concerns because of very different worldviews and world visions. A simple little tract about Jesus is not likely to suffice. The question becomes, how can you witness to people with a New Age worldview, values, and vision?

FOLLOW PAUL'S EXAMPLE

In a post-Christian and post-theistic age, follow the example of Paul's approach to evangelism, not Peter's. Peter's Jewish hearers had been taught the Old Testament from childhood, were theists, and knew that the personal, covenant-making God of Israel had predicted the coming of the Messiah. On the day of Pentecost all Peter had to do was to show how Jesus fulfilled those predictions in order to affirm that he was both Lord and Christ (Acts 2). Unfortunately, most Christians try to use a "just quote the Bible" approach for everyone. As Walter Martin has said, "We have to know enough about the people we are reaching to know which verse to quote!" Furthermore, we need to quote a relevant passage with understanding and with love. Otherwise our words will be empty.

In working with New Agers we cannot assume understanding of the personal, living, and active God, nor of his revelation, the Bible. In this regard our mission is much more like that of Paul, the apostle to the Gentiles or pagans (1 Tm 2:7). The Gentiles were heathen who did not worship or serve the personal God of creation or biblical revelation. Today most of the people we seek to reach for Christ have little acquaintance with the covenant-making God of the Old Testament. Outreach to New Age people in particular cannot assume accurate biblical knowledge. So we can learn much from the major passage explaining the approach of the apostle chosen of God to reach non-theists like the Stoic pantheists. The Stoics thought the *logos* was an unchanging principle of change (like evolution) within the world.

Like Paul, *be observant.* While waiting for members of his missionary team in Athens, Paul saw that the city was full of idols (Acts 17:16). He reported that he looked carefully at their objects of worship (v. 23), or examined them as a doctor would a patient. Missionaries must examine the culture and religion to be reached.

With your friends and relatives influenced by New Age approaches to life, promote understanding and just relationships. Christians treat fairly those with whom they differ. They represent their views honestly. We need not and ought not exaggerate New Age beliefs or practices, but we may acknowledge our desires for holistic health, achievement of our full potential, uplifting thoughts, spiritual growth, and world peace.

Like Paul, *be concerned.* As a result of what Paul learned he "was greatly distressed" (v. 16). Paul's righteous indignation is similar to that of the Lord when Israel, so recently delivered from Egypt, worshiped a golden calf. Paul could have been carried away by the aesthetics of some of the world's finest sculptures of Greek gods and goddesses. One writer says that in Athens there were more gods than men! The acropolis stood in all its beauty and centuries of destruction had not taken their toll. While doubtlessly moved by the beauty, Paul was angered by its idolatrous significance. When studying the New Age movement we may be impressed by some of the superficial aspects, but deeply distressed by its deep devotion to idolatrous causes.

Like Paul, *be conversational.* Paul, filled with the Holy Spirit, was able to control his indignation and "reasoned in the synagogue with the Jews and the God-fearing Greeks, as well as in the marketplace day by day with those who happened to be there" (v. 17). Paul engaged in friendly two-way conversation (dialogue) with idolators, Epicurean naturalists (like secular humanists), and Stoic pantheists (like New Age pantheists). By this daily demeanor Paul earned the right to be heard further and aroused the curiosity of philosophers and others who always wanted to hear something new. Christians will not be able to reach New Agers for Christ if they do not keep open channels of communication.

Your friends and relatives may be involved in the New Age movement to very different degrees and may, or may not, be involved in some of its practices. So it is important not to assume that you know what every New Ager believes or does. Talk with each person you seek to reach individually. Inquire about their values, what they consider important and worthwhile. Find out especially their ultimate concern. What is their *summum bonum* (highest good)? What is their *raison d'etre* (reason for existence)?

Similarity of wording may be expected. Ask questions to be sure you understand what your friends and relatives mean by the words. When they affirm belief in God, Christ, or Scripture, do not be satisfied. Ask for definition of meanings. What, more specifically, do they mean? If that is not clear, ask for further explanation.

What are your friends' points of agreement and difference with essentials of Christian faith? Some Christians acknowledge only differences with other faiths. Overlooked may be the possibilities of some truth from universal revelation in nature and the human heart.[5] Also they may overlook previous contact with Christian ideas. At the other extreme are those Christians who acknowledge only agreements with our faith, imagining that all religions teach the same way of life. For the sake of intellectual honesty, if not objective scholarship, we must honestly evaluate both similarities and differences. So, as you talk with New Agers, *be ready to affirm agreement where that is possible with understanding*. Be ready also to point out conceptual differences where necessary, avoiding merely verbal controversies.

Set apart ideas from the persons who hold them. Although for over thirty years I have strongly opposed the teachings of pantheism and occultism, I seek to respect the rights of people influenced by these views and to love them as Christ would. "Concern for persons in the lives of the apostles did not imply the compromise of doctrine. And a wise communication of Christian truth need not be uncaring."[6]

Like Paul, *be tactful.* When Paul stood to address the distinguished leaders of the famous city-state, the Areopagus, did he say, "You apostate philosophers"? No, Paul's approach was not judgmental. Did he say, "Now my dearly beloved brothers"? No, Paul's approach did not assume that all religions had the same values or world vision. He addressed the distinguished group of civic leaders like a board of education or supreme court, with respect. Paul used the usual terms of address for the position, "Men of Athens" (v. 22). However strongly we may differ with New Age friends and relatives, we need to respect them as persons in the image of God with inherent human rights to believe what they will.

Like Paul, *find something to commend.* Paul said, "I see that in every way you are very religious" (v. 22). In contrast to naturalists, New Agers may be commended for realizing that there has to be something more. There is more to life than meets the eye of the materialists. (Eastern European countries in rebellion against their Communist dictators are demonstrating that there is more to life than meets the eye of Communist dialectical materialism.) New Age people want spiritual experience. Some of them may be more faithful in their spiritual disciplines than we are. Paul similarly could speak of his Jewish friends as "zealous for God" (Rom 10:2), but he regretted to add, "their zeal is not based on knowledge" and the desire of his heart was that they may be saved (v. 1).

Like Paul, *"pray in the Spirit* on all occasions" (Eph 6:18). Presumably Paul's approach to the Athenian idolators, pantheists, and naturalists was saturated with prayer in the Spirit (Eph 6:18). He asked others to pray for him repeatedly in his letters and prayed night and day for his converts. In his walk Paul kept in step with the

Spirit, was led and filled with the Spirit. The Spirit had providentially prepared him for this great encounter of Jerusalem with Athens. Behind the scenes Paul knew that he struggled not merely with superstitions, philosophies, and religions, but "against the rulers, against the authorities, against the powers of this dark world and against the spiritual forces of evil in the heavenly realms" (Eph 6:12).

Christians seeking to win any to God's kingdom must understand that like Paul they also do battle with the kingdom of darkness. Any who would reach out to New Agers therefore must prepare thoroughly, putting on all God's armor for defense: truth, righteousness, a peaceful readiness, and the shield of faith to extinguish all the flaming arrows of the evil one (Eph 6:10-17). Offensively, witnesses to New Agers need sharpened skills of "fencing" with the sword of the Spirit and praying in the Spirit on all occasions (v. 18). Only so equipped and trained will we have the Spirit of love, wisdom, grace, and power to help New Agers leave the kingdom of darkness for the kingdom of light.

WHAT NEW AGERS SEEK

New Agers are often disillusioned naturalists or secular humanists seeking something more than meets the scientist's eye or than materialistic success involves. As the subtitle of Marilyn Ferguson's The Aquarian Conspiracy states, New Agers are people who seek personal and social transformation.[7] Unfortunately, many have also had disillusioning experiences in unfruitful Christian churches. So they turn away from churches for new spiritual experience, knowledge, and power.

Feeling estranged from the major secular and religious elements of a western society, New Agers long for meaningful relationships and commitments in new ways. Robert N. Bellah and others in Habits of the Heart: Individualism and Commitment in American Life[8] appreciates the desire for community among isolated Americans in general and the New Agers' need in particular. Part of the reason for the success of the New Age movement in America is that it addresses this general need of the culture for loving relationships and meaningful community. Effective approaches to New Age people will exemplify as well as describe the superior virtues of an Evangelical Christian approach to loving relationships and meaningful community.

New Agers seek loving relationships among themselves and value love highly, as do Christians. A convert from the New Age movement writes, "We need to understand that the vast majority of the people involved in the New Age movement are there because of deep emotional pain. Many have experienced the stifling rigidity, legalism, and lovelessness of a Christianity that was devoid of the real love of Jesus Christ."[9] Without love all our efforts to reach New Agers will be ineffective (1 Cor 13:1-3). God has not called us to be self-righteous, but to be sensitive to people's needs, to listen to them, and accept them as they are. The most effective ministry comes out of personal relationships. When you have taken time to build a relationship with a New Ager, your witness is more likely to be well received.

"Many have never experienced the love of God through another person, or seen God's character expressed in their neighbor's words and deeds. The media don't tell them the truth about God, their families haven't known him, and their schools have left him out of the curriculum. When you encounter someone in the New Age, never underestimate your value as a messenger of God's love and truth."[10] Friendship evangelism has been found to be one of the most effective ways of gaining permanent converts to Jesus Christ.

In witnessing, generally avoid the hard cases, Elliot Miller suggests, and *seek out those hungering souls who are ripe for the gospel.*[11] At New Age events like psychic fairs in shopping malls there may be many who are seeking something more and do not know that they need the Lord. As a New Ager, Elliot Miller "would lay awake at night tortured by the insanity of being a purpose-seeking creature in a universe which either lacked purpose, or whose purpose was beyond finding out." On LSD and other drugs, however, he received "revelations." After reading some of these revelations to a friend, the friend said, "My God, Elliot, you've turned into Christ!" Elliot admitted possibly being a prophet since he received revelations. Later he received a premonition that a new truth would soon be revealed to him. While on a lonely Southern

California beach feeling in perfect harmony with the universe, his privacy was broken. He recalls,

> The girl came over and sat in front of me, silently smiling. "Wow, I'm really stoned," I said—hoping for an understanding response. "Jesus really loves you, brother," she replied.
>
> My mind reeled. Was *this* the new truth that would challenge my commitment to follow truth? For years I had been *thoroughly* convinced that no one who really understood modern knowledge could believe in a supernatural Jesus. Furthermore, the Christian lifestyle seemed as unattractive as any I could think of. I was therefore both confounded and shaken by this revelation. How far was I to take it?
>
> Joining us, the girl's boyfriend expounded the same old evangelistic "pitch" I'd heard many times before from the mouths of "Jesus freaks"—young converts mostly from the drug culture. In the past I'd been impossible for them to reach. But this time when he asked me to pray with him and receive Jesus into my heart, I remembered my commitment to flow with and not resist whatever happened that day. So I joined him in prayer, and whereas I'd been "peaking" on the drug a few minutes earlier, its effects were now almost imperceptible. . . . Whereas earlier I'd serenely sat there in yogic, "full lotus" position, I was now on my knees, beseeching God to reveal to me the significance of the evening's events.[12]

The direction of Elliot Miller's life changed that evening. He is now the author of *A Crash Course on the New Age Movement* and edits the *Christian Research Journal.*[13] In the process of understanding and addressing particular New Agers' needs at the time, we may need also to reintroduce them to the Lord of all who can meet our deepest need.

LIKE PAUL, CLARIFY WHO GOD IS

The issue with New Agers is not the existence of God, but what God is like. Like the ancient Stoics, New Agers think of God as the unchanging principle of change within nature—"evolution" in

New Age thinking. With people ultimately concerned about an impersonal energy of the Force, evangelism begins with who God is. People are not likely to call upon God to save them if their God cannot hear or answer prayer. Unless we clarify the meaning of "God," our New Age friends who hold some form of pantheism (all is God and God is all) will not understand how God the Father could send his only begotten Son that they might have eternal life. New Agers tend to think that Jesus is God as all humans are alleged to be. Unless we define our terms, their apparent agreement with our affirmation of Christ's deity may mask a failure to affirm that Jesus alone is from above, all others are from below. Unless we clarify that God is personal, our New Age friends cannot appreciate the offensiveness of sin—rebelling against one who loves them. Unless you clarify that God is love, New Agers may think you refer to their Platonic principle of cosmic love. The ultimate reality is not a powerless Platonic idea, nor a qualityless void, but a living, active Spirit who is love, holiness, and all the other attributes Scripture assigns to him. Love is not above God, beside God, or beneath God; love is an essential eternal characteristic of the living God.

In other words, Christian witnesses to non-theists need to do what Francis Schaeffer called "pre-evangelism" or what is generally called apologetics. Christian witnesses to New Agers need to be ready to give a reasoned defense in support of their theistic worldview (1 Pt 3:15). In contrast to pantheists who think God is all and all is God, theists hold that God is a personal spirit distinct from the cosmos but active in it. The issue is not whether God exists, but whether the Christian theistic or the New Age pantheistic view of God is closest to the nature of the highest reality with which we have to do.

THE LOVING CREATOR UPON WHOM WE ALL DEPEND

Help your friends and neighbors realize that God is *distinct* from the world (Acts 17:24-28). God is changeless, the world is changing. God is independent, the world is dependent. God is holy, the world fallen. If God is the world or is in the world's being, God is indistinguishable from evil. Does it matter if people worship Mother Nature? That is like asking if it matters whether you love your spouse or just your spouse's artistic productions. To worship and serve the creation more than the Creator is sinful idolatry (Rom 1:25). Help your friends and relatives realize that the whole cosmos depends upon one who is distinct from the cosmos.

Your New Age friends cannot understand the gospel unless they understand that God is a *personal spirit* (Jn 4:24). And God wants a loving relationship with us in spirit and in truth. An impersonal energy does not provide as adequate an explanation of either the fact or value of personal human existence. Only against a personal God can your friends understand their sin. Only a personal God can pronounce a verdict of guilt and judgment. Only a personal God can create personal agents responsible for their thoughts, desires, and actions.

Your New Age friends also need to grasp the fact that God is a *living and active* spirit-being. Because impersonal, "the Force" (for example, atomic energy) cannot respond to persons. Impersonal psychic energy similarly does not know, care, or do anything for us personally. Scripture makes it clear that anyone who comes to God "must believe that he [a personal spirit] exists and that he [actively] rewards those who earnestly seek him" (Heb 11:6).

THE SOURCE AND SUPPORT OF ALL VALUES
TO WHOM ALL ARE ACCOUNTABLE

The New Age god is beyond good and evil, a-moral. Having had guilt feelings under earlier Christian influence, New Agers feel relieved of any sense of sin in their new faith. We must help New Agers come to understand that the living God upon whom they depend for their life and breath is *moral*. The living God is the source of all that is worthwhile for our well-being, the "Father" of all humans' metaphysical existence (Acts 17:28). But that does not make us God's children or brothers and sisters morally. The Holy One is removed from all that is destructive of body or spirit. God is by nature opposed to all that is immoral or unjust. Having created us in his likeness, God holds us accountable for disobedient moral thought, desires, decisions, and behavior.

In our culture it becomes increasingly evident that all fallen people need accountability. Presidents, legislators, judges, law enforcement people, those in health services, teachers, students, administrators, managers and laborers, all must give account of their abilities and resources. In naturalistic and pantheistic worldviews the cosmos or its inner energy is impersonal, so there is no One to whom to give account. But deny it or not, they are accountable to the Holy One.

Witnessing in any heathen culture requires pre-evangelism or apologetics like that of Paul's to clarify who God is, the One on whom all depend, and to whom all are morally accountable.

HELP NEW AGERS ACKNOWLEDGE THE BASIC HUMAN PREDICAMENT

In ways appropriate to the understanding of the one you seek to reach, you will need to answer the New Age claim that our deepest problems are not moral, but metaphysical. New Agers generally believe that, for some unknown reason, we human "emanations" from the one universal spirit began having illusions. We have *imagined* that we are distinct from God, when in fact, we have all emanated from the divine being. So our basic need is to overcome all this illusory, conceptual, and scientific thinking by meditative techniques to convince ourselves that we *are* divine. We need union or fusion with the One. Since in the final analysis all is one, evil is no different from good! New Age people are not likely to seek forgiveness of sins if all sins are thought to be illusions.

Our deepest problems are not metaphysical, but moral and relational. God wants to use you to help your friends realize that according to Christ and Scripture *our deepest problems are not metaphysical, but moral and relational.* Our need is not union, but communion. We were created distinct from God, although in God's likeness for fellowship and fulfilling work. We broke God's wise counsel and became estranged from God, guilty before divine law and disabled by intractable moral evil. Never will God call our evil good or good evil! Before the judgment of divine justice, we are all found guilty.

We must deliver the divine summons to all New Agers everywhere to repent. Paul did not hesitate to call on sinners in the great Greek culture at Athens to repent. Christians today need to recover a sense of the sinfulness of sin. Then we need to help New Agers realize the inescapability of moral accountability. Repentance is not an elective, it is a command. We must *deliver the divine summons to all New Agers everywhere to repent* (Acts 17:30). Like all who are born of the flesh (Jn 3:6), New Agers must turn from their unfaithfulness to their creator and sustainer. They have blurred the distinction between creature and Creator, resulting in sinful idolatry (Rom 1:25). They have loved the architect's work and depersonalized the architect of the cosmos. Above all else, God wants their love. God created persons not to absorb them in an impersonal vat of energy, but to enjoy personal fellowship with them throughout time and eternity. Our unique identities survive death and face judgment. You will be judged, not for what others (in other alleged lives) have done, but for what you have done with your opportunities in this one lifetime.

Announce to New Agers the day of judgment (Acts 17:31). It is a clever perennial deception that we have countless lives in which to evolve spiritually or accumulate good karma. We live once and we die once (Heb 9:27). If there were other lives in which the reincarnate could get right with God, how unlike the loving Jesus not to let us know! Instead, he illustrated the joy or pain faced after death in the account of the rich man and Lazarus the beggar (Luke 16). Jesus taught that people settle their eternal destiny in this one lifetime (Mt 25:46). Paul wrote, "Now is the day of salvation" (2 Cor 6:2). The urgency of decisions for Christ in the New Testament can only be explained on the basis of the crucial opportunities in this one life.

History had a beginning and it will have an end. So does each unique life. Distinctively human existence is linear and once-for-all, not endlessly cyclical. Death is far from unreal, it remains the ultimate enemy of human existence on earth. The inner person, the spirit, separates from the body and goes to be either with Christ in joyful celebration or forever removed from Christ in hopeless despair.

New Agers will then face judgment by Jesus Christ, not by an endless evolutionary development. The basis of our hope under the penetrating rays of divine judgment is not our spiritual evolutionary development, but our reception of Christ's atoning provisions. The best of us is far from morally perfect. But God is holy and demands perfect karma. In heaven, ninety-nine is not a passing grade! No single sin can be admitted there. As Paul argued, "if righteousness could be gained through the law, Christ died for nothing" (Gal 2:21).

The goal of pre-evangelism has been reached if our friends realize that the Lord of all transcends the world in power and morality, that they have but one life and it will soon be past, and that they face divine judgment alienated, condemned, and depraved.

Listen prayerfully in order to address a particular point of need adroitly as did Jesus and Paul. A pastor in Hawaii befriended a New Age couple who lived together without marital commitments. The woman knew that she should try to feel mature about an open marriage in accord with New Age relativism. She knew that her "husband" who traveled frequently on business trips need not be faithful to her. Although she kept telling herself that she was now mature, she could not stand the thought of his being with another woman during his time away from home. To overcome her unloving attitudes she would take another New Age course. *A Course in Miracles* helped for a while, but it did not erase her desire for fidelity. The same problem kept returning over several years after numerous courses.

Out of inescapable dissatisfaction with the New Age ethic the couple talked with this wise pastor who assured her that God approved of her value of faithfulness. She was greatly encouraged to hear that she was right. But still she could not forgive her mate. The pastor then prayerfully and lovingly confronted her with her unforgiving spirit. She came to admit her bitterness and called upon the living God to forgive her and help her become forgiving. Meanwhile, her mate was so moved that he in turn for the first time in his life prayed to God. He asked God for help to be faithful to her. God enabled him to overcome the desire for other women. On his next business trip the desire for the other woman who was also along did not recur. Upon his return the couple enjoyed an unhindered relationship; each made commitments to Christ and to one another. The pastor had the joy of baptizing and marrying them on the same day! They now give their testimony that the power of the gospel is greater than the powers of the New Age. The potential that could not be realized by countless New Age courses over some fourteen years was found as they turned over their lives to Christ.

After people are aware of their need for a higher personal power, their need for repentance and for God's forgiveness, the task of pre-evangelism has prepared the way for the task of evangelism.

PRESENT THE GOOD NEWS PROVIDED BY THE ONCE-FOR-ALL INCARNATION, DEATH, AND RESURRECTION OF JESUS CHRIST

Our task with heathen men and women culminates like that of the apostle to the Gentiles in reporting the good news that a just amnesty is possible because the Messiah has come! Jesus Christ provided the gift of total amnesty at present and at the final judgment for all who will accept it. The amnesty is just because he suffered in our stead. The demands of justice for our greed and lusts have been paid in full. On that basis believers are not only forgiven of their sin but also given the perfect righteousness of Jesus Christ. Furthermore, they are reconciled to God's fellowship and redeemed from addictions to moral evil.

As the Lausanne Covenant defines it, "To evangelize is to spread the good news that Jesus Christ died for our sins and was raised from the dead according to the Scriptures, and that as the reigning Lord he now offers the forgiveness of sins and the liberating gift of the Spirit to all who repent and believe. . . . Evangelism itself is the proclamation of the historical, biblical, Christ as Savior and Lord."[14]

New Agers typically may need help to understand *the uniqueness of Jesus' incarnation.* Jesus is not just one of many gurus who have passed along the wisdom of the sages as a great teacher and example. Jesus was the eternal Word of God (Jn 1:1) who became flesh and dwelt among us (1:14). New Agers regard Jesus highly as a man ordinarily born who realized his inner divinity and became God. Many world religions present leaders who came to be regarded as divine. Christians alone, in contrast to all others, worship a God who became a man in order to seek and to save the lost. The Christ of the Bible knows, hears, answers, judges, and saves. "Yet to all who received him, to those who believed in his name, he gave the right to become children of God—children born not of natural descent, nor of human decision or a husband's will, but born of God" (Jn 1:12).

New Agers may also need to realize that Jesus was not one of many such gurus, but unique in his life. Jesus had not studied the world's wisdom, yet he spoke with authority. Unique in his character, neither close friends nor arch enemies could find any fault in him. Even Judas said, "I have betrayed innocent blood." Jesus performed miracles that made a difference in history. No one ever taught with the authority of Jesus. Jesus even predicted his own death and resurrection. "Just as man is destined to die once, and after that to face judgment, so Christ was sacrificed once to take away the sins of many people: and he will appear a second time not to bear sin, but to bring salvation to those who are waiting for him" (Heb 9:27-28). Jesus is the unique, once-for-all deliverer. We live once, not many times, and after death we face judgment. We will not be judged by Krishna, Gautama, Socrates, Plato or Aristotle, the Maharishi Mahesh Yogi, or Shirley MacLaine. We will be judged by Jesus Christ.

New Agers may wonder how Christ's death affects their moral status. Since Jesus did not sin, he did not need to pay the penalty of sin—death. But he willingly chose to suffer death for others. Christ's *death once-for-all provided his perfect righteousness as a gift.* New Agers may think that they need to earn good karma and they need to help others to earn good karma. The beggars in India pursue people in order to help them earn good karma by giving alms. The Christian who is asked to contribute to a New Age cause for that purpose might reply, "Thank you for trying to help me earn good karma. Did you know that I have perfect karma? United with Christ by faith, his perfect righteousness has been imputed to my account! And you can receive the gift of perfect righteousness here and now." Concerning the Jews who similarly tried to be saved by keeping law, the Scriptures explain: "Since they did not know the righteousness that comes from God and sought to establish their own, they did not submit to God's righteousness. Christ is the end of the law so that there may be righteousness for everyone who believes" (Rom 10:3-4). Your New Age friends need to accept the perfect righteousness that God gives.

Christ's death also provided for our *reconciliation to fellowship with a personal God.* However far from a holy God New Agers may seem to be, like the prodigal son, they may return to the heavenly Father. The cross of Christ assures any New Ager that the Father's longsuffering has not come to an end. God's love still awaits the turning, the conversion of those who were seduced by pantheism.

How do we know that Christ is the unique judge and transformer of human hearts? "God has given proof of this to all men by raising him from the dead" (Acts 17:31). The multiple converging lines of historical evidence overwhelmingly support *the fact of Christ's resurrection.* For forty days Jesus appeared to women and men, disciples and ordinary people, to doubting Thomas, and to Saul who became Paul. The sealed and guarded tomb was empty. The bodies of all the founders of the other world religions remain in their tombs. Death, they discovered, is no illusion. Christ's tomb alone has been emptied.[15] Christ has ascended to heaven far above all angels and demons. Jesus Christ alone today is able to transform any New Ager who calls upon him in sincerity and truth.

The New Agers' quest for *world peace* is worthy indeed. World peace is a goal Christians also seek. Ours is not a fatalistic utopia such as promised by the Marxists' dialectical materialist philosophy. Neither is it a visionary and unrealistic bit of wishful thinking. Knowing the fallen nature of human beings, Christians know that, as Plato said in *The Republic,* no human is either wise or good enough to be trusted with power over the world. The history-transcending, risen Christ alone is able to bring a lasting and just peace to this fallen world. Jesus explained that there would be wars and rumors of war until he returned (Mt 24:6). Then he will be the King of Kings and Lord of Lords (Rv 19:16) and will reign a thousand years (20:4-6) with peace and justice for all. The dream of New Agers for world peace can best be realized not by turning to magical manipulation of alleged psychic forces but by faith in the one who defeated moral evil on the cross and conquered death by walking triumphantly out of his tomb.

Only the God who is living and active above the world and able to guarantee a conclusion to history in which justice triumphs over injustices of all kinds can fulfill New Age hopes for world peace. Invite your New Age friend to trust the living Lord Jesus Christ as disclosed in Scripture.

MORE HELP FOR THE EVANGELIST

For additional ways to clarify the gospel to New Agers who talk about the Bible, Jesus Christ, the cross and resurrection, see my book *Confronting the Cults*. I went through the New Testament to see what it says we must believe in order to have eternal life. Seven questions bring out these convictions and outline the chapters on Christian Science, Unity, and Spiritualism (or channeling), and others. After ·indicating answers from the standard literature of these groups, I explain how to help people from these perspectives understand the gospel of grace.[16] My book, *What Everyone Should Know about Transcendental Meditation*,[17] uses five questions to help clarify the frequently blurred distinctions between Christianity and the New Age. But for even more extensive material differentiating central Christian beliefs from those of the New Age movement, see *Integrative Theology* vols. 1 and 2.[18]

Additional help for Christians facing the problem of making the gospel clear will come from defining key terms. For this we can make use of the old catechisms and recent works in Christian theology that interact with New Age ideas.[19] We must know our God and how to clarify his uniqueness from the cosmos. We must know Scripture and reasons for its reliability over channeled guidance from finite, fallible spirits of alleged spiritual masters. We must know Jesus Christ and why he is not just one more *avatar* or *guru*. The tragedy is that many Christians are ill-prepared to deal with the claims of those who are non-Christian.

How do you reach people who have rejected all other ways of knowing reality and consider their own interpretations of their own experiences to be the ultimate authority? I vividly recall the difficult experiences of trying to help a Denver University law student reach his wife, who was "blissed out" as a devotee of Guru Maharaj Ji. This daughter of a Wycliffe missionary couple became committed to the Guru and taught in his school. At the peak of an impressive counterfeit experience, it may be impossible to reach some New Agers. We may have to watch and pray, until like the prodigal son they come to their senses (see Lk 15:17). Until then keep loving channels of communication open. And we will want to be ready to give them a warm welcome when they become disillusioned with their counterfeit spiritual masters and seek the one at the right hand of God in heaven.[20]

Obviously there is not a single simple formula for reaching people caught up in New Age intuitions, assumptions, and experiences. Hopefully the proposed approaches here will help those who want to do something for their friends and relatives.

THROUGHOUT BE YIELDED TO THE HOLY SPIRIT

We will not fulfill our Lord's great commission in our own wisdom or strength. When Christ ascended to heaven, he promised to send his Spirit. On the day of Pentecost the apostles were "filled with the Holy Spirit" (Acts 2:4) and were subsequently filled several times (4:8; 7:55). We are exhorted to be filled with the Holy Spirit (Eph 5:18). Only the Holy Spirit can transform human hearts. To enter the kingdom of God people must be born from above. Without yieldedness to the Spirit, Christians are like cars without fuel.[21] Each of us needs to rely totally on the wisdom, grace, and power of God's Spirit to bring forth fruit. We must convey the fact that Christ gives us an abundant life. A vibrant life based on truth will commend the faith.

New Agers seek not just knowledge but also power to overcome their present limitations. They may turn from their spirit-guides when you can illustrate the richness of Holy Spirit-guidance in harmony with the Word. The Spirit who raised Christ from the dead can deliver New Agers from frustrations, anger, hurts, and emptiness. The Holy Spirit can deliver from the power of evil spirit-guides. The appeal of the New Age occultism is not only in hidden knowledge but also in secret power. Powerless Christians will have little effect in witnessing to New Agers. Christians who dabble in occult phenomena themselves are in no position to help New Agers find deliverance. Christians giving ground in spiritual warfare are not ready to witness to New Agers. We are ready for front line spiritual warfare only when we have become well equipped with Christ's righteousness, peace, and salvation.

RESULTS

Whatever you do, some New Agers may mock your advocacy of the living God and moral law. Some mocked our Lord and some sneered at Paul (Acts 17:32). Others may put you off saying, "We want to hear you again on this subject" (v. 32).

But several may become followers and believe in Jesus Christ (v. 34). Two of the converts were well enough known to be named—Dionysius and Damaris. And others were converted. That is phenomenal success! Given an audience of educational and political leaders, the fact that *any* trusted Christ is evidence of the powerful way the Holy Spirit worked through Paul's message.

APPEAL

The mission fields are now divided not only geographically but also sociologically in terms of unreached groups of people with a given affinity.[22] The New Age mission field is composed of people with spiritual affinities unreached by the gospel and of essentially nominal Christians who still attend church.

Christian mission boards need to recruit and send out missionaries to people who are seeking spirituality in non-Christian ways. One mission board open to applicants for missionary service to New Agers is the Conservative Baptist Home Mission Society in Wheaton, Illinois. And Denver Seminary has a department preparing people for service to new religions and cults.

God forbid that followers of Jesus fail to fulfill their Lord's great commission! New Agers are working night and day to fulfill theirs.

FOUR

The Unification Church

James A. Beverley

A UGUST 20, 1985, was an important day for Rev. Sun Myung Moon. In the early morning hours he was released from prison after serving thirteen months for income tax evasion. On that same day, at 6:00 P.M. in Washington, D.C., he was guest of honor at a God and Freedom Banquet attended by seventeen hundred clergy from many denominations. Moon was greeted as a great Christian leader and as a courageous champion over injustice.

Rev. Moon views his time in the Danbury, Connecticut federal prison in a positive light. Speaking to his own members on August 29, 1985, he declared: "My victory at Danbury also has meant my own resurrection, both physically and spiritually. I am now in the position of Lord of the Second Advent to the world. . . . Much confusion and chaos prevailed before I entered prison. But with my emergence as the victorious Lord of the Second Advent for the world, a new order has come into being."[1]

The term "Lord of the Second Advent" is the Unification wording for Messiah. Rev. Moon claims to be the fulfillment of the second coming predicted in the New Testament. Moon's imprisonment and subsequent announcement of his Messianic role are just two indications of the immense controversy surrounding him and his Unification church.[2]

How does Rev. Moon's life and message relate to the gospel of Jesus Christ? Do members of the Unification church need to hear an evangelistic appeal from Christians? If so, how does one evangelize a Moonie?[3] What is the Christian response to the ideology of the Unification church?

Like their founder Rev. Moon, Unificationists are accustomed to controversy. They tolerate attempts at evangelistic witness but they find it frustrating. One could hear from them statements like the following: "Don't you know that Rev. Moon received his mission from Jesus Christ himself in Easter of 1936?" "Even our official church title shows the positive role we play since we are The Holy Spirit Association for the Unification of World Christianity." "We believe the Bible, love Jesus, and want to follow the Holy Spirit." "We are on the same side, serving the same God. Why do fellow Christians want to burden us with their evangelistic outreach?"

While this ecumenical appeal must be noted, it demands careful scrutiny too. False gospels do not advertise as such, and the mere claim to like-minded belief and practice does not constitute proof. But doesn't Rev. Moon deserve some benefit of the doubt? Dr. Milton Reid, one of the pastors at the God and Freedom Banquet, said that the Korean leader is "perhaps one of the most misunderstood religious leaders since Jesus of Nazareth."[4]

A proper attitude to evangelism of Unificationists depends, of course, on a fair and accurate understanding of Rev. Moon, his beliefs, and his followers. To that end some attention needs to be given to the history of the Unification church and to the central teachings of the Unification theology.

BRIEF HISTORY OF THE UNIFICATION CHURCH

Though some religions can be understood with little regard to the life of the founder, such is not the case with either Christianity or the Unification church. What are some essential elements about Rev. Moon's life that can introduce us to the history of his church?

Sun Myung Moon was born on January 6, 1920 in Pyung Buk-do, now part of North Korea. Moon was raised in the Christian tradition (with both Presbyterian and Pentecostal influences) and allegedly received a revelation from Jesus Christ at the age of sixteen. From 1936 until the end of World War II, Rev. Moon prepared for his mission and was given fresh insight into the meaning of the biblical revelation. He knew that he was called to bring a new ideology that would allow democracy to conquer Communism, and in the late 1940s and early 1950s Rev. Moon underwent incredible suffering for his faith and courage. He was imprisoned because of his anti-Communist views and his strength during years of persecution inspired an early group of followers.[5]

The Unification church was officially founded in 1954. A mission to Japan started in 1958 and the next year Young Oon Kim (recently deceased and the most significant Unification theologian) was sent to America.[6] Rev. Moon did not attract worldwide attention until his own personal mission to the United States in the early 1970s. He became famous for his public defense of Richard Nixon. Rev. Moon has held giant rallies at Madison Square Garden (1974) and at the Washington Monument (1976). He has also mobilized his followers into political action against Communism, chiefly through the CAUSA organization.[7]

Moon has also tried to influence the media through establishing newspapers in the Orient and also in New York and Washington, D.C. There was much controversy over the launching of *The Washington Times*, with questions asked about Moon's influence and financial power.[8]

Rev. Moon studied electrical engineering at Waseda University in Japan, and the movement values learning and scholarship. For example, the Unification Theological Seminary was founded in 1975 at Barrytown, New York, and the church plans to have an international university in Korea. Rev. Moon has also sponsored numerous conferences for scholars working in various disciplines.

Undaunted by the lengthy criminal procedures against him in the early 1980s, Rev. Moon continues to reach out as a spiritual leader to the world. He recently granted an interview with a Russian newspaper to announce his friendship with the Soviet people and to declare his optimism about the work of Mr. Gorbachev.[9] In April 1990, Rev. Moon met privately with President Gorbachev in Moscow.

Three things need brief comment. First, the controversy and media attention surrounding Rev. Moon often hide the fact that he has relatively few followers in North America. Second, it is easy to be seduced by the rhetoric of success. The Unification church excels in public relations and the life of Moon is made to sound like a fairy tale come true. Third, an account of Unification history and Moon's life should pay attention to the serious questions that must be asked about the origins of the church and about the current realities in the personal life of Rev. Moon.

CENTRAL UNIFICATION BELIEFS

The central task in forming a Christian response to the Unification church is to evaluate the message of Rev. Moon in the light of biblical revelation and the historic Christian faith. On this point, the radical break of Rev. Moon from classical Christianity must be emphasized. It is difficult to overstate the discontinuity between the gospel of Jesus Christ and the vision of Rev. Moon. It cannot be Jesus Christ and Moon; rather, it is Jesus Christ *or* Moon. In defense of this verdict, note the following summary of Unification beliefs.

First, Unification theology offers a *new revelation*. This revelation is in the person of Rev. Moon and in his text *Divine Principle*. That two-fold revelation is captured by the following claim from the movement's central holy book.

With the fullness of time, God has sent His messenger to resolve the fundamental questions of life and the universe. His name is Sun Myung Moon. For many decades, he wandered in a vast spiritual world in search of the ultimate truth. On this path, he endured suffering unimagined by anyone in human history. God alone will remember it. Knowing that no one can find the ultimate truth to save mankind without going through the bitterest of trials, he fought alone against myriads of Satanic forces, both in the spiritual and physical worlds, and finally triumphed over them all. In this way, he came in contact with many saints in Paradise and with Jesus, and thus brought into light all the heavenly secrets through his communion with God.[10]

Second, Unification theology offers a *new Messiah*. Jesus Christ was the first Messiah for the New Testament age and Rev. Moon is said to be the Messiah for the Completed Testament Age. The book *Divine Principle* is an extended attempt to prove that both the New Testament and subsequent events in history point to the rise of the Messiah in Korea shortly after the end of World War I.[11] The second coming of Christ does not demand, so Unificationists would tell us, the supernatural, personal return of Jesus. In point of fact, Rev. Moon holds a higher position than Jesus Christ, second only to God the Father. God loves Moon more than the whole world, and more than Jesus Christ as well.[12]

Third, from the above, it follows that Unification theology offers a *new understanding of Jesus*. Contrary to classical Christianity, the Unification church denies the Trinity, the virgin birth of Christ, and the bodily resurrection of Jesus. Further, church members (sometimes called Moonies) teach that the unbelief of John the Baptist and other Jews forced Jesus to die on the cross instead of following the ideal mission of finding the proper wife and becoming a true father to a lost world.

Jesus' death on the cross brings only spiritual salvation, not physical redemption. God the Father had to wait for Rev. Moon to complete the failed mission left behind by a crucified Jesus.[13] The role of Jesus in eternity will be secondary to that of Moon. In fact, Moon even asserts that his deceased son Heung Jin has a higher place than Jesus in eternity.

Fourth, Unification theology offers a *new view of the Fall of mankind*. Eve was seduced into sexual intercourse with the devil. She then had intercourse before due time with Adam. Her adultery with Satan produced Cain and her premature sex with Adam resulted in Abel. History has been a battle ever since between the Cain and Abel lines. Our blood lineage can be traced ultimately to Satan, and it is the task of Rev. Moon to indemnify or pay for all the past sins of mankind.[14]

Fifth, it is clear that Unification theology offers a *new view of salvation*. To the Moonie, Jesus Christ is not the final and ultimate Savior of the world. His death on the cross is not sufficient to give complete salvation. The death of the second Adam (Jesus) does not offer full atonement. Rather, for full salvation God has sent a third Adam (Moon), who by his sinless life and perfect marriage offers full redemption and perfection.

On March 16, 1960, Rev. Moon married Hak Ja Han, then a young

Korean woman of seventeen, and theirs is the heavenly union predicted in the Book of Revelation and called the Marriage Supper of the Lamb. Moon and his wife and children constitute the True Family and through them the kingdom of heaven will be brought to earth.[15]

Sixth, Unification theology offers a *new view of eschatology*, including a form of universalism that teaches Satan's ultimate restoration. Unificationists are open to the major religious traditions, though Rev. Moon's life and teaching provides the ideal of truth and righteousness. Further, the Korean prophet will be the main standard on Judgment Day. He has unlocked all the secrets of the universe, and to defy him is to defy self, posterity, one's country, the world, and God. In heaven, Westerners will want Rev. Moon in their homes and bedrooms, and the guards at the gates of heaven will admit people on the basis of their physical resemblance to the Korean leader.[16] Korean will be the heavenly language, and one's place in the afterlife will be measured in part by one's knowledge of Moon's mother tongue.

Finally, Unification theology offers *new ritual in worship and religious life*. For example, Rev. Moon has initiated a new calendar of holy days for their church year, and there are distinctive elements in their Sunday worship services. Further, members are given elaborate instruction on proper use of Holy Candles, on the best attire for holy services, and even on the proper way to bow to True Parents. Members are advised on the value of carrying Moon's picture with them as a protective measure.

On a more esoteric note, Unification members use Holy Salt (created by Moon on his wedding day) to bless their food, their homes, and their offices. Moon also created a new kind of Holy Wine that is taken by disciples at their initiation into membership. Rev. Moon has also blessed various geographical sites around the world and these Holy Grounds are often the locale for special prayer and worship.[17]

It would be unfair to restrict this brief note on ritual to overtly religious activities and items. Rev. Moon encourages his followers to bring the Unification vision to every area of life. Thus Moonies are involved in a whole range of educational, political, and social programs.

RESPONSE TO UNIFICATION THEOLOGY

A. Crucial Practical Strategies. These suggestions are not radical or new but they are the very items so often forgotten in witnessing.

1. Every Unificationist is to be addressed in a *loving manner*. This does not mean that a milk-toast attitude to their ideas is justified but all too often Evangelicals care too little about a loving interaction with followers of other faiths. Moonies have often experienced incredible love and support in their church.[18] That reality needs to be applauded and Christians must emulate such love in their midst and in their evangelism.

2. Every Unificationist is to be affirmed in *freedom of religion*. Tell the Moonie that you defend his or her right to believe in Rev. Moon and to accept the teachings of *Divine Principle*. This is not a ploy for effective dialogue. Rather, it is a recognition of the fundamental liberty that should be granted to all humans, including cult members.

3. Unificationists are to be treated as *individuals*. Moonies are not robotic clones! It may surprise you but there is a real diversity among Unificationists. They are far less uniform than one might expect, certainly far less predictable than followers of some other cults. Some Moonies are quite fundamentalist in religious outlook. They would no more challenge Rev. Moon than some Christians would challenge Jesus. Other Moonies would have radical doubts about even the most basic and central Unification claims. In dealing with individual followers of Moon, it will do well to remember the wisdom behind the slogan "different strokes for different folks." Your witness should vary according to the needs and realities of those you seek to reach.

4. Unificationists are to be *commended for every good and decent reality* in their faith and living. It is counterproductive to decry everything about a given cult as if it is all error, sin, and total darkness. No, the Unification church has strengths for us to affirm, and members can be praised for the virtue and goodness in their lives. It is no shame or scandal to admit that Rev. Moon has some ideas worth hearing. For example, he often preaches about the compassionate heart of God, and that is a tremendous theme for orthodoxy to emphasize.

5. Unificationists are to be viewed as *sincere followers* of their faith.

This does not mean that their way is truth. However, nothing is gained by assuming that Moonies must be crazy or insincere simply because they follow Moon. Think for a moment how successful the Unification church looks to its membership. Theirs is a worldwide following. Rev. Moon has achieved international fame for his leadership. Moonies are persecuted for their faith. They have a rich diversity of programs in education and culture.

Beyond this, many Moonies would offer you strong and compelling testimonies about the dramatic impact that Rev. and Mrs. Moon have made on them. Their witness has a ring of spiritual power and transformation. Here, for example, is one testimony about Mrs. Moon. "Her face shines with a radiant, inner happiness which, I believe comes from the fulfillment of love. Perhaps that is the greatest, deepest gift which Mrs. Moon has given me—she has shown me a true mother's love, and in doing so, has given me an example to follow in my own life. Words can teach us many things, but by example Mrs. Moon has truly enlightened my life."[19] This kind of personal witness must not be dismissed out of hand. Evangelicals must be sensitive to the complex realities at work in the faith story of others, even those in groups ultimately opposed to the heart of the gospel of Jesus.

B. Crucial Christian Critique for Evangelism. With the above points firmly in mind, the following response to the Unification worldview is suggested for evangelism of followers of Rev. Moon. Hopefully these crucial elements in the Christian critique of Unification ideology will be used by the Holy Spirit to bring Moonies to the light of Jesus Christ.

1. There is to be no retreat from the reality that *Unification theology is unbiblical.* Many of the teachings of Moon do not agree with the clear teachings of the Old and New Testaments, the authoritative Scriptures for the Christian church. It is *not* simply an issue of interpretation at this point, as if any view must be tolerated as equally worthy of assent by Christians.

For example, Rev. Moon teaches that Zechariah is the father of Jesus. The adulterous relationship of John the Baptist's father with Mary produced severe tension between Mary and Joseph, Moon tells us. This in turn caused Joseph to resent Jesus and consequently Joseph and Mary deliberately left twelve-year-old Jesus behind at the temple in Jerusalem! This theory makes no place for the traditional teaching of the virgin birth (see Matthew 1:18 and Luke 1:34-35), nor does it fit with the plain teaching of the Gospel account: "After the Feast was over, while his parents were returning home, the boy Jesus stayed behind in Jerusalem, *but they were unaware of it. Thinking he was in their company, they traveled on for a day"* (Lk 2:43, 44).[20]

2. Evangelicals should realize that the Unification church *denigrates the person of Jesus Christ.* Moon's displacement of the centrality and uniqueness of Jesus Christ is done, he assures us, in the name of Jesus, even, we are told, at the request of Jesus to Moon in 1936. However, authentic evangelism demands that Jesus be esteemed in the same manner as portrayed in the New Testament. The theory that Rev. Moon is the second coming of Christ is an outright denial of the clear New Testament teaching that it is Jesus himself who will return in triumph (see Acts 1:11).

3. Careful reading of Moon's sermons illustrates another factor for use in evangelism. Rev. Moon engages in *prophetic speculation* but fails in the process. His sermons in the 1970s predicted that by 1980 the Unification church would own a fleet of 747s for international travel. He assured his followers that Communism would be overcome by 1980, and he told of the end of persecution by 1981.[21]

4. An evangelical witness to Unificationists will also take note of *implausible* and *egocentric* views of Rev. Moon. The Korean prophet claims to be God's "only champion." He states that he has no example to follow, that he is the leading foe of Communism in the world, that the U.S. fishing industry depends on him for survival, and that Reagan would have lost the 1984 presidential election if Moon had opposed him. In one sermon Moon asked: "What if I did not exist?" His answer: "It would be as if all the world were here but were empty."[22] Claims like these demand rational scrutiny, as does the Unificationist belief that Moon's deceased son Heung Jin was elevated from prince to king in the spirit world through a post-mortem, proxy marriage on earth.[23]

C. Conclusion. Members of the Unification church labor under a heavy burden, that of obeying the ever-changing and never-ending demands of their master. Christians must not despair in their desire to evangelize Moon's disciples. Under the burden of Moon's lordship the invitation of Jesus will perhaps bring a word of hope to the individual Moonie. For Jesus said: "Come to me, all you who are weary and burdened, and I will give you rest. Take my yoke upon you and learn from me . . . and you will find rest for your souls" (Mt 11:28, 29).

There is further cause for hope. Followers of Rev. Moon are idealistic visionaries. They are people who know what it is to sacrifice for a cause. They are committed to changing the world. With some optimism, then, the Christian can ask Moon's followers to reconsider the wonderful, liberating claims of the gospel and give their total and undivided allegiance to Jesus Christ, the only Messiah of the eternal God.

Mormonism

Wesley P. Walters

WITNESSING TO MORMONS is not an easy task. Seldom does one lead a Mormon, a member of the Church of Jesus Christ of Latter-day Saints, to Christ at the first encounter. One should be ready for some lengthy conversations over a considerable period of time before the Mormon will be ready to abandon his beliefs for a personal relationship with Christ.

WITNESSING WITH THE BIBLE

The most natural way to begin witnessing to a Mormon is to use the Bible. However, this is fraught with difficulties. First, Mormons have been taught that the Bible has been badly damaged and is, to a good degree, unreliable. The Mormons' Eighth Article of Faith says they believe the Bible "insofar as it is correctly translated." Taken at face value, this is an acceptable statement. No Christian wants to base his faith on a verse of the Bible that is mistranslated. However, Mormons stretch this statement to mean that in places the Bible has not been correctly *transmitted.* Anywhere the Bible clearly does not agree with present Mormon doctrine, they will claim that it has been damaged in transmission. If one is not careful, the whole discussion can turn into a two-hour debate on how reliable the Bible is.

Pastor Ira Ransom, a long-time missionary to the Mormons, found this happening with great frequency. Finally, he hit on the idea of beginning any discussion by asking the Mormon, "How reliable is the Bible?" He had them tell him where they thought the Bible text was unreliable, and he promised to avoid those passages. Usually the Mormon was unable to cite a single reference, but if he or she could think of one or two, he simply noted them down and agreed to avoid them. This enabled him to get directly to the Bible without a lengthy argument.

A second problem which a Christian faces in using the Bible with a Mormon is the matter of the Mormon's own inner "testimony." This is basically a *feeling*, a "burning in the bosom," that assures him or her that Mormonism is true, that Joseph Smith, its founder, is a prophet, and that the Mormon church is the only true church. Because of this, Pastor Ransom found that often when he made a point clear from the Bible, the Mormon would fall back on his "testimony" ("I want to testify by the Spirit of God that I know Mormonism is true,") and the whole point was lost. Pastor Ransom again solved this problem by dealing with it up front. Before beginning any discussion from the Bible he asks: "In your search for truth, which is more important, the Bible or your feelings?" He encourages them to choose the Bible by reminding them that Proverbs 14:12 says that "there is a way that *seems* right to a man, but the ends thereof are the ways of death." On the other hand, Jesus has assured us that heaven and earth would pass away but his Word would never pass away (Mk 13:31). Once the Mormon has agreed to the principle that the Word is more basic than feelings, if he should at some point fall back on his "testimony," Mr. Ransom simply reminds him that he is expressing his *feelings*, but they had already agreed to focus on the Bible, and he returns to the passage at hand.

A third problem a Christian faces in using the Bible with a Mormon is the redefinition of terms. Mormons have given their own content to familiar terms in the King James Bible (the Bible version they officially use). For example, when a Christian speaks of Christ's "atonement," he understands this to mean the sacrifice on the cross that removed the guilt of all our sins so we can be brought back into fellowship (at-one-ment) with God. To the Mormon, however, atonement means the death of Christ that only cancels out Adam's sin and therefore guarantees to everyone a resurrection. (A list of such changes in meaning is given at the end of this chapter.) With such altered meanings, it is often like speaking to each other in two different languages. One way of breaking through this is to avoid these familiar King James expressions which they misuse and adopt another rendering. For example, wherever the King James Version uses "grace," substitute "undeserved favor" when reading the verse. Search through several modern translations until you locate substitute wording you can feel comfortable with, and stick to those renderings.

Once one has gotten over these initial difficulties, many Christians who are experienced in talking with Mormons think the best place to begin is with the Bible's teaching about God. The Bible and Mormons are clearly at odds at this point. The Bible teaches quite plainly that there is only one God. Mormons, on the other hand, teach that three separate gods rule our planet—the Father (Elohim), the Son (Jehovah), and the Holy Ghost. The Father and the Son have physical bodies of flesh and bone as tangible as a man's, while the Holy Ghost has a body of spirit (*Doctrine and Covenants* 130:22). ("Spirit" in Mormonism is less dense, more refined, thinned-out matter, like a gas.) In addition, Joseph Smith taught that the Father (Elohim) has a father and a grandfather God, for our own Father God had once been a man on another planet ruled by *his* heavenly Father. After faithfully obeying all the Gospel laws and ordinances, and being married to a wife (or wives) for eternity, he died, was resurrected, and was exalted to godhood. He now rules this, his own planet, on which we, his children, born of his wife, live. Every Mormon man who follows the same path can expect to become a god like Father Elohim, and organize and populate his own world. This process has been going on eternally, so there are billions of gods throughout the vastness of space, although Mormons are told to concern themselves only with the three gods who rule our planet.

It should be very clear to even the most inexperienced Christian that this is not the view of God taught in the Bible. One can see why Mormons want to regard the Bible as severely damaged in transmission. Otherwise their strange ideas about God would immediately be seen as gross error. However, many Mormons are not well enough acquainted with the Bible to know precisely what the Bible does teach about God. Therefore the Christian should show him plain and explicit verses. Since Mormons believe that all gods were men before they became gods, a good place to begin is with passages from Isaiah chapters 43 to 46. Isaiah 43:10 stresses that there were no gods formed before the Lord and there will be none formed after him. If that verse is true, then our God could not have had a Father and a Grandfather who became gods before him. Furthermore, no present-day Mormon male can hope to become a god if none are to be formed after the Lord.

Again, one might ask the Mormon if he believes God knows everything. Most will agree he does. Then take note of Isaiah 44:8 where the Lord asks, "Is there a God beside me?," and answers, "... there is no God. I know not any." If present Mormon teachings were true, how could the Lord not know of the existence of a single god beside himself? Continue on through chapters 44 to 46 and highlight all the places that declare there is no God besides the Lord. How many times does God have to tell us something before we believe him?

By contrast, the God who made this extremely complicated world of nature is certainly at least as complex, if not more so, than what he has made. This is why we find the nature of God presented in the Bible to be a very complex one. Christians have tried to express this by using the term Trinity (derived from *tri-unity*) meaning one God, but existing in a complex three-ness of Father, Son, and Holy Spirit (or Holy Ghost). This distinction of three-ness within God (some call it three centers of consciousness) is unfortunately referred to as the three *persons* of the Trinity. Early Christian writers who wrote in Latin struggled to find a term to use for this three-ness and hit upon the Latin word *persona*. *Persona* was a theatrical term meaning a role or character in a play. These characters were depicted by using different masks, and one actor could play several parts by changing masks and sounding his lines through (per-sona) the mask. *Persona* became the accepted term for referring to the three-ness within God. However, once the word *persona* gave rise to the English word "person," it unfortunately came to mean not a "role" or "character" but an "individual." Thus when Christians tell the man on the street that we believe in "one God in three persons," he thinks we are saying we believe in one individual who is three individuals, which to him is nonsense. So try to avoid the term "person," or at least explain that you are using it in its very ancient, technical sense.

Many have found Titus 3:5 a good starting point in presenting the gospel to Mormons: "Not by works of righteousness which we have done, but according to his mercy he saved us, by washing that comes through regeneration and the renewing that comes through the Holy Spirit." Since in Mormon teaching Jesus' death on the cross only cancels Adam's sin, the Mormon is on his own to work for his salvation. While Mormons do say that Jesus' death *makes possible* our forgiveness, this forgiveness actually is earned by our repenting. The Mormon Missionary Training Manual of a few years ago stressed that repentance means never indulging in the sin again, "not even in your mind." What a harsh view of repentance to consider that if the sin even enters your mind again you have not truly repented! This can be a very wearisome burden, with little relief offered from the guilt that comes through failure. Mormons are trying to develop the idea that when Christ agonized in prayer in the Garden of Gethsemane, "shedding as it were great drops of blood," he was making additional possible provision for our sins. But Paul made it very clear in the opening verses of 1 Corinthians 15 that the gospel was not that Christ *agonized* for our sins, but that he *died* for our sins—and it was for *our* sins, not just Adam's, that he died. This is the glorious good news we owe to every Mormon. Here is where the mercy offered in the Bible by a Savior, whose death cancels *all* our sins, offers such a wonderful hope to guilt-laden sinners.

WITNESSING WITH THE BOOK OF MORMON

A second method of witnessing to Mormons is by using the Book of Mormon. When Joseph Smith wrote it, he borrowed his theological ideas from the various groups in his area. From the Methodists he borrowed the idea of free will; from the Baptists the position that baptism should be by immersion; from the Christian Connection group the idea that the church should only be called by the name of Christ. Because of this borrowing, the book reflects a basic Protestant theology, close to some of the Protestant churches of our day. However, another result is that the theology of the Book of Mormon is greatly at odds with present-day Mormon teaching!

Pastor John L. Smith, a missionary to Mormons in Utah for thirty years, likes to open his conversations with Mormons by saying, "If I believed the Book of Mormon were true, I would have to believe your church is false; if I believed your church were true, I would have to believe the Book of Mormon is false." He can say this because the Book of Mormon differs so drastically from present Mormon theology in so many places.

Most obviously, the Book of Mormon's doctrine of God is monotheistic, while present-day Mormons are polytheists. For example, notice the conversation that the book depicts between Amulek and Zeezrom. Amulek opens the dialogue by stating that he cannot say anything contrary to the Spirit of God. This means that all the words that Amulek will say are virtually the words of God himself. Then Zeezrom asks, "Is there more than one God?" Amulek answers, "No." Zeezrom then asks, "How knowest thou these things?" Amulek replies, "An angel hath made them known to me" (Alma 11:22-31). One could hardly ask for a more clear and authoritative statement that there is only one God! This means that the current Mormon idea of many gods existing throughout all the extent of space is wrong. Numerous other passages reinforce this idea that there is only one God. Even the phrase, "the Father, Son, and Holy Ghost is one God," is several times repeated.

While this sounds like the orthodox Trinitarian teaching about God, the book elsewhere (e.g., Mosiah 15) shows that Smith had really adopted Sabellianism (or modalism as it is sometimes called) which some preachers in the county where he lived were teaching. Sabellianism holds that the words "Father," "Son," and "Holy Spirit" do not denote any real distinction within God, but are just modes of talking about God from our human vantage point. Thus when we speak about God in heaven, we call him "Father"; when we speak of him incarnate as Jesus, we call him "the Son"; and when we speak of him at work within us, we refer to him as the "Holy Spirit." Because the Book of Mormon adopts this erroneous view of God (Mosiah 15:2-5), it speaks as if there is no real distinction between the Father and the Son. Thus in Esther 3:14 (The Book of

Mormon) Jesus can appear on the scene and claim "I am the Father *and* the Son." In spite of this weakness, the book is still exclusively monotheistic, and as a result hopelessly at odds with present Mormon polytheism.

Another point of variance is the eternal existence of God. Moroni 8:18 asserts that God is "unchangeable from all eternity to all eternity." If God were once a man and became God, as present Mormon doctrine asserts, then he certainly would not have remained "unchanged from all eternity," and the Book of Mormon would have to be regarded as teaching falsehood about God. On the other hand, if the Book of Mormon teaches the truth about God, then present Mormon teaching that God changed from being a man into being a God must be false. The modern Mormon cannot have it both ways.

At other points the Book of Mormon teaching is also close to that of the Bible. The book asserts that when one dies he either goes to heaven or hell. In hell the torment is eternal (2 Nephi 9:16), although, unlike the Bible teaching, it is only the person's unending sense of guilt that torments him. In modern Mormonism, on the other hand, nearly everyone goes to one of three degrees of glory (based on an erroneous treatment of 1 Cor 15:46, 47). Many of the few that do go to hell are thought to get out after a thousand years and enter the lowest degree of glory. In the Book of Mormon there is no salvation after death (Alma 34:32-35), while a modern Mormon is encouraged to spend a good deal of time doing works to rescue the dead. This is the reason for their great emphasis on genealogy—so they can be baptized for, and thus rescue, their dead relatives.

In the Book of Mormon man has a sinful nature (Mosiah 3:19), while modern Mormonism emphasizes that man is a god in embryo. Because man is viewed as sinful, the Book of Mormon urges a spiritual rebirth, whereas the Mormon church today regards baptism into the church as being "born again."

One of Joseph Smith's early revelations claimed that the Book of Mormon contained the fullness of the gospel (*Doctrine and Covenants* 20:9). Can this be true when it leaves out such important present Mormon teachings as men becoming gods, marriage for eternity, works to rescue dead relatives, and a host of church offices, "ordinances," and "endowments" never mentioned in the book?

WITNESSING THROUGH CONTRADICTIONS

A third method of witnessing to Mormons is through the contradictions in their own words and writings. If one were to point out to a Christian five or six apparent contradictions in the Bible, it is doubtful that this would shake his faith in Christ and Christianity. If, however, one could show five hundred or more contradictions that involve important points of doctrine and belief, then serious doubts would arise. Similarly, one should not expect that showing a Mormon a few contradictions in his church's scriptures will make him haul up the white flag and surrender his faith in Mormonism. However, as the conflicts begin to multiply—as they do in Mormonism—to dozens and hundreds, then a Mormon's faith in his false foundation may begin to crumble, and he may be open to hear the good news about God's forgiveness in Christ.

When Bob Witte and Melaine Layton began the movement known as Ex-Mormons for Jesus, they sent out some questionnaires asking ex-Mormons what led them out of the Mormon church and into faith in Christ. Of the four hundred replies, some two hundred indicated that it was the internal contradictions and conflicts within Mormonism that first raised doubts about the truth of their beliefs and opened them up to consider the claims of Christ in the Bible. Therefore, a good grasp of a number of important conflicts can open a door for presenting the good news about Jesus.

One large group of conflicts concerns the changes Joseph Smith made in his own "revelations." Instead of writing new "revelations" when he changed his theological ideas and saying "Cancel the previous revelations!" he tried to work his later theology and ideas *back into* his earlier revelations and make it look as if they had been there all along. For example, he claimed to have received a revelation from God telling him he had received a gift to translate the Book of Mormon and he was to "pretend to no other gift, for I will grant him no other gift" (*Book of Commandments*, 1833.4:2). After finishing the Book of Mormon, however, Joseph decided that he wanted to revise the Bible. Two years after he finished this task, in 1835, when his revelations were republished, he changed this revelation to read "You have a gift to translate... this is the first gift that I bestow upon you... pretend to no other gift until my purpose is fulfilled in this, for I will grant you no other gift until it is finished" (*Doctrine and Covenants* 5:4).

Another very significant change in Joseph Smith's revelations concerns the "Law of Consecration." When the young prophet moved to Kirtland, Ohio, in 1831, he introduced the practice of having all things in common, as in Acts chapter 2, which he called "Common Stock." Accordingly he received a revelation from the Lord that every Mormon was to consecrate "*all* thy properties" to the church "with a covenant and a deed which cannot be broken" (*Book of Commandments* 44:26). Under this plan a person signed over all his property to the church and was loaned back enough items (dishes, plow, etc.) to live on. The rest of his property was loaned to those who had no possessions of their own. If a person left the church, even the items loaned to him had to be returned to the church.

When this Common Stock plan proved unworkable, the Lord settled for ten percent, as a subsequent 1838 revelation made plain (*Doctrine and Covenants* 119). Consequently, when the original Law of Consecration was reprinted, God's demand was changed to read that a good Mormon should consecrate "*of* thy properties" (*Doctrine and Covenants* 42:30). Later at Nauvoo, when a man named John Finch came to town preaching communalism, the Mormon leader stated that he "did not believe the doctrine" (*History of the Church* VI:33; Smith's Diary, Sept. 14, 1843). He subsequently preached for an hour on Acts 2 "designed to shew the folly of Common Stock" (Diary, Sept. 24, 1843 [Signature Books ed. p. 415]). Today the giving of ten percent of one's gross income to the church is still demanded and is one of the indispensable requirements for admission to the temple, where alone one can be sealed in marriage for eternity and thus progress to godhood.

An airline pilot who likes to witness to Mormons carries with him in his flight bag photocopies of the revelations before and after they were changed. When he meets a Mormon he may say, "I just happen to have in my bag some copies of old Mormon documents, if you are interested." This gets their attention, and turns the conversation in a direction that undermines the Mormon's base of authority.

One of the most recent blows to Joseph Smith's claim of being a prophet with divine powers of translation was the resurfacing of some papyri he had purchased in 1835. He identified one of the papyri as the writings of Abraham, and proceeded to "translate" a history of Abraham's conflict with pagans in Chaldea, which is now a part of the Mormon scripture *Pearl of Great Price.* This is also the main source of Mormon teaching of the plurality of gods. The papyri were thought to have been long ago destroyed in a fire in Chicago, but they were discovered in 1967 in the Metropolitan Museum in New York. When the material was translated by professional Egyptologists, it was found to say nothing about Abraham, but to be directions to the embalmers on how to wrap the mummy and accompanying papyrus. For details on this whole incident, consult Harry Ropp's book *Are the Mormon Scriptures Reliable?*

There are numerous examples of such changes, conflicts, and cover-ups in Mormon writings and history. A massive array can be found in Jerald and Sandra Tanner's self-published *Mormonism: Shadow or Reality;* or in their greatly shortened version, published by Moody Press, *The Changing World of Mormonism.* Those who wish to witness to Mormons would do well to master presenting as many of these conflicts as possible.

In witnessing to Mormons, many blend all three methods—the use of the Bible, the use of the Book of Mormon, and presenting Mormon contradictions. However, in all the discussions one must be sure to stress the good news of God's forgiving love. There is much guilt that builds up Mormonism, even though their view of sin is rather low, and there is very little to offer forgiveness. To the Mormon the gospel is not wonderful good news of forgiveness and salvation in Christ, but is a series of laws and ordinances to be obeyed to attain godhood. They must keep all the laws of the Bible, the Book of Mormon, Joseph Smith's revelations in the *Doctrine and Covenants,* as well as the commands of the living prophet, the head of the Mormon Church of Jesus Christ of Latter-day Saints. These constitute thousands of laws. Where does one turn to gain forgiveness from such a burden of guilt? The teaching that Christ's death only cancelled Adam's sin and merely provided for the possibility of forgiveness, if one adequately repents, is not much help. We owe every Mormon the glorious good news that Christ died for his sins, not just for Adam's, and offers forgiveness and salvation to all who come to him by faith.

One ex-Mormon likes to go directly to the point by saying: "What is God doing in your life?" and then he proceeds to tell the Mormon what God has done in his life. Perhaps you may find this approach the easiest of all. But most Mormons are not so easily moved, and you need to master the above suggestions, and then get busy witnessing to your Mormon friends and neighbors. After all, the good news does not belong exclusively to you—you also owe it to them.

Helpful Aids to Witnessing

Barnett, Maurice. *Mormonism Against Itself* 2 vols. Louisville, KY: Gospel Anchor Publishing Co., 1980 (712 Victoria Place, Louisville, KY 40207). Reproductions of early Mormon documents, 8 ½" x 11," punched for three-ring binder.

Cowan, Marvin. *Mormon Claims Answered.* Salt Lake City (SLC): Utah Christian Publications, 1989 (Box 21052, SLC, 84121). A concise presentation of Mormon teachings and the passages they use to support them, along with a penetrating assessment of their errors.

Ropp, Harry. *Are the Mormon Scriptures Reliable?* Downers Grove, IL: InterVarsity Press, 1987. A handy survey of the flaws in Mormon sacred writings.

Tanner, Jerald & Sandra. *Mormonism: Shadow or Reality.* SLC: Utah Lighthouse Ministry, 1987. *The Changing World of Mormonism.* Chicago: Moody Press, 1980. *Major Problems of Mormonism.* SLC: Utah Lighthouse Ministry, 1980 (Box 1884, SLC 84110). Admittedly the best discussion of the conflicts and contradictions in Mormonism.

Tope, Wally. *On the Frontline.* La Canada, CA: Frontline Ministries, 1981 (Box 1106, La Canada Flintridge, CA 91011). A good summary of Mormon arguments, with some useful answers.

Witte, Bob. *Where Does It Say That?* Brockton, MA: Ex-Mormons for Jesus, 1986 (Box 2403, Brockton, MA 02403). Nearly two hundred pages of photo reproductions (reduced four to a page) of documents showing how Mormon doctrine has been modified.

Wood, Wilford. *Joseph Smith Begins His Work* vols. 1 and 2. SLC: Deseret Press (Available from Utah Lighthouse Ministries). A photo-mechanical reprint of the original 1830 *Book of Mormon* (vol. 1), and of the 1833 *Book of Commandments* and the 1835 *Doctrine and Covenants* (vol. 2).

Terminology Differences

PRE-EXISTENCE

Latter-day Saints (LDS)—Teach that everyone pre-existed—we all exist eternally.
Bible—Only Christ pre-existed—not man (Jn 8:58; Col 1:17). We didn't have a spiritual existence prior to earth (1 Cor 15:46).

FALL

LDS—Teach it brought mortality and physical death—not fallen nature—believe Adam was given two conflicting commandments and was supposed to fall.
Bible—God tempts no one (Jas 1:13-14). Man is basically sinful (Rom 8:5-8; 1 Cor 2:14).

SIN

LDS—Specific acts—not man's basic nature.
Bible—We are in spiritual rebellion until conversion (Eph 2:3; Rom 5:6). We do not just commit sins—we are basically sinful (Mt 1:21).

REPENTANCE

LDS—Repent of individual acts—not sinful nature.
Bible—Must repent of basic rebellion (Jer 17:9; Lk 5:32).

ATONEMENT—SALVATION BY GRACE

LDS—Believe Christ's death brought release from grave and universal resurrection—salvation by grace is universal resurrection—beyond this man must earn his place in heaven.

Bible—Salvation is not universal but is based on the belief of each individual (Rom 1:16; Heb 9:28; Eph 2:8-9).

REDEEMED

LDS—From mortal death only—not sinful rebellion or spiritual death.

Bible—Christ redeems from more than mortal death—redeems us from spiritual death (Rom 6:23; Eph 2:1).

GOSPEL

LDS—Mormon church system and doctrines.

Bible—Message of Christ's death and resurrection as atonement of our sins (1 Cor 15:1-4; Gal 1:8).

BORN AGAIN

LDS—Baptism into LDS church.

Bible—We are spiritually dead until our spiritual rebirth (1 Pt 1:23; 2 Cor 5:17).

TRUE CHURCH

LDS—Only Mormon church—true church taken from earth until Joseph Smith restored it.

Bible—As born-again Christians we are part of God's church (1 Cor 12:12-14; Mt 18:19-20; Mt 16:18).

AUTHORITY—PRIESTHOOD

LDS—Believe only LDS have authority to baptize, ordain, etc.—

Have two-part system of priesthood—Melchizedek and Aaronic.
Bible—Christ brought end to Aaronic priesthood and is *only* High Priest after manner of Melchizedek (Heb 5:10).

BAPTISM

LDS—Must be performed by LDS priesthood.
Bible—Emphasis is on believer—not priesthood authority (Mk 16:15-16).

SONS OF GOD

LDS—We are all literal spirit children of God.
Bible—We become children of God at conversion (Jn 1:12).

ETERNAL LIFE

LDS—Exaltation in Celestial Kingdom—ability to bear children in heaven—must have a temple marriage.
Bible—Not limited to certain ones in heaven—no mention of parenthood or temple marriage but is given to all Christians (1 Jn 5:12-13).

IMMORTALITY

LDS—Universal gift—ability to live forever but not eternal life.
Bible—Makes no distinction between immortality and eternal life (2 Tm 1:10).

HEAVEN

LDS—Divided into three kingdoms—Celestial, Terrestrial and Telestial—place for almost everyone (misuse 1 Cor 15:40-41).
Bible—Only mentions two conditions—everlasting punishment or life eternal (Mt 25:31-46).

KINGDOM OF GOD

LDS—Means Celestial Kingdom—only those in Celestial Kingdom are in God's presence. Those in Terrestrial or Telestial Kingdoms aren't in presence of Father.

Bible—All redeemed will be in God's presence. (Rv 21:1-3). All believers are part of kingdom (Mt 13:41-43).

HELL

LDS—Hell as an institution is eternal—inmates come and go as in jail—don't spend eternity there—stay until one has paid debt to God.

Bible—No mention of people getting out of hell (Rv 21:8; Mt 13:24-43 and 47-50; Lk 16:26).

GODHEAD

LDS—Father God is a resurrected man with physical body, Christ is a separate resurrected man with physical body, Holy Ghost is a separate man with a spiritual body—three totally separate gods.

Bible—God not a man (Num 23:19). Only one God (Is 43:10-11; 44:6; 45:21-22). Father is Spirit and invisible (Jn 4:24; 1 Tm 1:17).

HOLY GHOST

LDS—Is a separate God from Father and Son—different from Holy Spirit—Holy Ghost is a person—Holy Spirit is influence from Father and not personal.

Bible—Same Greek word used for *Holy Ghost* and *Holy Spirit* (1 Cor 3:16 and 6:19).

VIRGIN BIRTH

LDS—Believe God, as a resurrected, physical man, is literal Father of Jesus—same manner in which men are conceived on earth—believe Mt 1:18 in error.

Bible—Says Mary was "with child of the Holy Ghost" (Mt 1:18).

Courtesy of Sandra Tanner, Utah Lighthouse Ministry.

SIX

The Occult

Karen Winterburn

AN ASTROLOGER'S ADVICE

"I feel like a bird trapped in a cage I can't see!" My voice cracked; I cried. I was grateful to be able to share my discouragement with this sensitive and insightful astrologer. Although I had been a professional astrologer for several years by this time, I sought this man's counsel to help solve my spiritual frustration.

"I can see from your chart that you are being driven to God, Karen. You are bound to find the path to divinity that is right for you."

"That's just it!" I insisted. "I can only get so far on any of these paths and I come up short. I just can't break through with any of these gods." We'd been talking about experiencing one's own divinity through devotion and submission to such "god-manifestations" as Buddha, Isis, Shiva, Pallas Athena, and Ithursis, an entity I was channeling.

The astrologer looked intently at the piles of my chartwork which covered his desk. I was convinced my answer was encoded in there somewhere and that he was about to decode it for me.

"What's your religious background?" he asked, without looking up.

"Christian," I said.

He looked up abruptly. "What do you think about Jesus Christ?" he asked point-blank.

I was irritated and offended. "What do you mean by that?" I snapped. "I don't know what I think about him. What difference does it make?"

He shuffled all my papers into one pile as though there was nothing more to say. "Until you know what you think about Jesus Christ and come to terms with that one way or another, you won't be any good to Buddha or Shiva or any other god. Your spiritual journey is blocked right here."

That was an astrologer's advice to me before I came back to Christ and committed my life to him. What a contrast with the lack of advice I received from most Christians I knew! Some were impressed and romanticized my strange "spiritual journey." Other responses ranged from morbid curiosity to polite silence. Tolerance abounded, and I never heard the gospel. So God used an unbelieving astrologer, himself a follower of pagan gods, to tell me that I needed to come to terms with Jesus Christ.

ARE YOU SURE?

God wants his people to share with others—including occultists—the truth he has revealed to everyone in his Word. This is the heart of evangelization. But to do this, we have to be sure of that truth ourselves.

A good place for us to start in evangelizing is to examine our own commitment to the truth and to the authority of Scripture. For instance, I can think of five things revealed about God in the Bible and five things revealed about man. I ask myself: Are these truths? Which of them would I stand up for? Which would I uphold in the face of social discomfort or worse? Does my daily living spring from a fundamental certainty regarding these truths? My daily living springs from *some* such certainties. What are they? Are they consistent with biblical truth?

Being certain that some particular things are true is a far cry from having all the answers. A defensive, know-it-all attitude on my part is occasion for the occultist to ignore *what* it is I have to say or to break off the relationship. Still, genuine certainty of biblical truth is an important component of witness. I can be an effective witness only to what I am certain is true.

If I am not certain of the absolute superiority of Jesus Christ over both the imaginary and the real spiritual entities worshiped in occultic religion, I'm useless in evangelism. But it is the superiority and authority of the living person Jesus which is the issue; not the superiority of Christianity, nor of the church, nor the Christian tradition, nor even less of the "disputable matters" of doctrine and conduct (Rom 14:1). This distinction is important, because witnessing to an occultist is a lot like being a foreign missionary. We have to be able to lay aside even legitimate religious elements of Christianity in order to present the person of Jesus Christ.

If, on the other hand, I believe that all men worship the same God, but in different ways, and that it is necessary only for Christians to worship him in Jesus, then the God I witness to is not the God of the Bible. If such is the case, I can never witness to the truth, but only preside over its suppression (Rom 1:18-20).

OCCULT BELIEFS AND THE BIBLE

As an occultist, I was constantly impressed with how all occult traditions and the ideas behind all occult practices tied together so neatly. It seemed as though they were all like spokes on a wheel. They appeared, from the rim of the wheel, to be separate, but they all led to the same center of hidden (occult) truth.

I studied and practiced astrology and many forms of divination and psychic reading, past-life regression, "altered states of consciousness," and spiritism, especially "channeling." I studied Eastern philosophy and yoga, primitive religions and "new" religions. I was convinced these were all hidden (occult) paths to God. They were all different, but they did not contradict each other. The most important beliefs and assumptions in each were identical. This happy fact was common knowledge among cultists. It bound us together and was the basis of our occult ecumenism.

The only "loose end" was Christianity. And we all knew it. The one task that we all had in common was the task of neutralizing the Bible and co-opting Jesus Christ into our various occult systems. The person of Jesus is a stumbling block for every occultist. We all tried to sneak around him, jump over him, or tunnel under him rather than face the fact that his teaching was incompatible with ours. We wanted Jesus to be another spoke on our wheel, leading to the center where "All is One."

In order to fashion this kind of Jesus, we had to deny the accuracy of the scriptural record of him and twist that record until it portrayed a Jesus who supported our teaching.

An effective Christian witness will keep the occultist honest about his failure, to co-opt either Jesus or the Bible. He will be able to demonstrate the integrity and the plain meaning of the Scripture so that the occultist will no longer be able to distort its message, but will have to accept or reject it. Evangelizing occultists is as much about building walls as it is about building bridges.

A good witness will also need to know something of occult beliefs. It's not necessary to know the detailed beliefs of every occult system, but rather the basic elements they have in common. These basic beliefs contradict and distort biblical revelation in every case.

"MAN IS AUTONOMOUS"

This was not so much a belief I assented to as it was an impulse that I cultivated and surrendered to. Occultists are determined to attain perfect human autonomy, to "ascend the throne of the Most High."

This contradicts the biblical principle of divine sovereignty. The God of Genesis 1:1 is an omnipotent Creator who created the heavens and earth from nothing, i.e., not from out of himself. He is distinct from his creation and sovereign over it.

But it was not his identity as Creator which was originally challenged. It was rather his sovereignty over creation. ("Eat this apple, and you can be in charge!") It was not disagreement over an idea, but disobedience to a command that generated the occult alternative. Human autonomy is the foundational ethical principle of occultism.

"ALL IS ONE"

A second belief common to occult systems is that each person or thing in existence is, in the last analysis, identical to every other person and thing in existence. Every *thing* that exists is a facet of the One Single Thing that exists. All is One. This idea is called "monism." Most occultists take this idea one step further and say that this One Single Thing that exists is Spirit or God. This is called "pantheistic monism" (*pan* = all, *theos* = God, *monism* = one).

Pantheistic monism is the typical worldview of occult and magical systems. In it, Creator and creation are illusory distinctions that are absorbed along with all other distinctions into the One. This is in contrast to biblical theism which recognizes the Creator as distinct from, and of a different order of being than, his Creation.

The occultist may not know the philosophy of monism, but an experience of it is built into his religious practices. My channeling experience, which lasted over a year and a half, began to convince me that my individual identity and personality were quite arbitrary. Other "individuals" claiming to be "higher facets" of me used my mind and body to express themselves. It seemed as though I had no personal boundary, and "Karen" was a mere convenience. The entities speaking through me assured me of this. I was identical to my husband, my children, the redwoods, the dolphins and every other person or thing that ever was. I thought that I could experience *being* any of them. I began to devalue *myself.*

This is the same thing that happens in rites of spirit possession and totemic identification within the religions that support more primitive cultures. These religions are becoming increasingly more popular in the West. Occultists with Western, Christian backgrounds are in many cases reviving and replanting these religions. Your next-door neighbor who's experimenting with the ouija board may get her consciousness altered to just the right frequency to tune into something like the African religion of Santeria.

Santeria is an example of a ready-made religion that Western occultists can move right into. In Santeria, All is One. *Ashe,* or power, does not reside in the gods. And it certainly doesn't reside in a distinct, sovereign, personal God. It pulsates through everything and everyone as the impersonal force moving them toward an impersonal end in the All.

Ashe is current . . . that initiates can channel. . . . The prayers, rhythms, offerings, tabus of santeria tune initiates into this flow . . . (this) world of power where everything is easy because all is *ashe,* all is destiny.... The real world is not one of objects at all, but of forces in continual process. ..."[1]

Santeria has *ashe,* Taoism has *chi,* and Hinduism has *prana.* All these religions are occult religions based on power. Biblical religion is based on ethics. Power religions engender both magic and a-theism. Ethical, theistic religion, when vigorous, resists them both.[2] Power religion cultivates the use of and identification with an impersonal, a-moral, evolutionary energy. Biblical religion holds one accountable to a personal, sovereign God.

"MAN IS DIVINE"

The third basic occult belief is that man is divine. Occultists believe that the apparent distinction between God and man is temporary and illusory. Everyone is or is becoming God. Consequently there is no distinct human nature, no natural limitations. When I came back to the Lord, I was relieved and overjoyed to be able to admit to the limitations of human nature. Scripture asserts that man is distinct from God and subject to him by virtue of his creaturehood. Our freedom is limited by his authority (Gn 2:16, 17).

Occultists believe that personhood is an illusion to overcome. There is no such thing as personal limitation. But I learned over the years that we can deny personal limitations only at the risk of losing touch with reality. It was actually invigorating and empowering for me to face my personal limitations again after my occult experience. I delight in being limited by my individuality. I can appreciate in a new way that I am a personal being, made in the image of a personal God in a special act of creation (Gn 1:27). This limits me. I cannot be anyone else, least of all my Creator!

To the occultists, human history is the process of mankind reclaiming its divinity. The perfect portrayal of this idea is found in the inner meaning of the myth of Osiris in the Egyptian mystery religion. The story of Osiris is anything but a resurrection myth! Osiris is a mythical king whose dismembered body was scattered far and wide, each piece in a different place. Through her magical powers, his wife Isis finds all the pieces and "re-members" them into a unified body in which Osiris attains divinity. The Egyptian initiate and the occultic initiate today identify themselves and all of manifest reality with Osiris.[3] Each sees himself as part of a dismembered God, which when "re-membered" through proper rituals will regain or finally gain divine consciousness. Osiris' human birth is said to be the birth of the god Ra himself,[4] not in the sense of the biblical doctrine of the incarnation, but because of the essential interchangeability of personal identities, divine or otherwise, within occult systems.

Occult groups provide initiation for their members into this "experience of divinity." It doesn't take long for a person dabbling in the occult to stumble upon one of these groups and get hooked up with it. These groups include black and white witchcraft covens, Satanic covens, full-scale revivals of ancient pagan religions (Egyptian, Chaldean, Roman, Greek, etc.), transplants of spiritualistic, animistic, or polytheistic religions of other cultures, or New Age groups formed to practice the teachings of some modern occultists.

My astrology teacher and mentor confided in me that she was a priestess of an ancient Egyptian god. She showed me her vestments, chalices, and other liturgical paraphernalia. Her role was recognized and practiced within a growing group of people in the Chicago area who were reviving the ancient Egyptian religion. It was a secret in the process of "coming out," the occult in the process of joining the mainstream.

Her initiation into the experience of her divinity was a tightly scripted scenario determined according to ancient specifications and astrological timing. It involved her spending a particular night in the sarcophagus of an Egyptian pharaoh. She traveled to Egypt solely for this purpose: to be "baptized" into the death of a god-king!

It seemed to me at the time, from the little I could recall about Christian teaching, that Christian baptism was a copy of this original. I assumed that the deeper, hidden meaning of Christian baptism must be to bring one to an experience of his divinity. This assumption helped assuage the uncomfortable feeling I had that I was straying far from my Christian roots.

It wasn't until much later, after I'd come back to the Lord and begun reading Scripture with new eyes, that I understood this occultic initiation as the counterfeit of biblical regeneration. Ritual initiation is produced by a magically symbolic death and rebirth. Biblical regeneration is produced by the sovereign will of a personal God at the point of faith commitment on the part of the person. The biblical act of baptism is not ritualistic in the magical sense. It dramatizes our identification in Christ, but does not produce it. And the identification it dramatizes is not an identification of our nature with his, but an identification into his position and standing before the God to whom we are accountable.

Occult "divinization" occurs through the gradual possession of the initiate by a personification of the divine. This is achieved through mind-altering, trance-inducing technologies such as drugs, ritual dances and physical exercises, sensory deprivation, meditation geared to shut down the rational mind, and verbal exercises designed to dismantle logic as a mental instrument. The Christian life, by contrast, is a process of "reflecting" or "contemplating" the Lord's glory, and so being transformed into his likeness (2 Cor 3:18). This is an interpersonal encounter leading to character transformation. I no longer await the fulfillment of my godhood, but with my brothers and sisters I await the fulfillment of our adoption as sons and the redemption of our bodies (Rom 8:23).

"IT'S ALL IN THE MIND"

The fourth principle of occultism is its method of dealing with human problems. Like the Bible, occultism gives a diagnosis of the human condition, offers a cure, and suggests a prognosis based on the cure. According to the occult diagnosis, human problems stem from ignorance. We are ignorant of the fact that we and all of nature share the same impersonal identity in the One. We are ignorant of our own divinity, and so we wrongly create exclusivistic identities, exclusivistic nationalities, and exclusivistic religions.

During the twelve years in which I believed this, I had the same kinds of personal problems and stresses common to many young working wives and mothers. I thought these were due to the fact that I had not yet learned to exercise the powers that lay hidden in my own nature.

I learned much later that the Bible points to sin—our hostility and indifference toward God—as the ultimate source of all our relational problems (Mk 7:20-23). We refuse to be accountable to God and so we blame each other as Adam did Eve (Gn 3:12). We're prepared to destroy each other rather than submit to God, as Cain responded to his brother's example of righteousness by killing him rather than by repenting of his rebellion (1 Jn 3:12).

Like Adam and Cain, I wasn't about to stop rebelling against God and start submitting to him. This made it all the more difficult for me to recognize and deal with the hostility and indifference which overflowed into my relationships with others. Like Adam and Cain I wasn't about to take on any unhealthy "guilt trips"! I was sure my problems would dissolve as I came to a fuller realization of my own divinity and learned to exercise the powers proper to it.

In order to attain such "enlightenment" and experience my divinity, I investigated a number of organizations founded in Eastern religions, primitive religions, and "new religions" or cults. I was looking for a guru. I finally settled on Church Universal and Triumphant, based on the channeled teachings of the "ascended masters" of turn-of-the-century Theosophy. Elizabeth Clare Prophet was its *Guru-Ma*.

Enlightenment is achieved through exercises which manipulate the mind and spirit. This is best facilitated through the intensification of the *guru-chela* (master-slave) relationship. This is a highly formalized, impersonal relationship between the initiate and his teacher which is characterized by the absolute submission of the initiate to the guru as the key context in which the mind-control and thought-control exercises of that particular tradition are carried out.

In order to bring this elusive enlightenment down to earth, I also sought practical occult knowledge which promised me power to change and control my daily circumstances. I thought I could solve marital conflicts by discovering how my husband and I were related in "past lives" and what kind of karma or consequences those past relationships created for us in this life.

I thought I would truly understand my children and coworkers and be able to relate to them constructively if I studied their astrological charts and treated them accordingly. If the solution to human problems was a change in consciousness, then I would willingly change mine. I made every effort to interpret the details of my life in the light of astrological cycles and my own and others' "past lives." I acted out of that view of reality on a daily basis.

The actual effect of living this out over the years was destructive. It placed severe and unrealistic limitations on how I could perceive people and interpret or evaluate their actions. By the same token, it destroyed those other limitations that were consistent with reality. It also restricted my own range of responses in an arbitrary and unrealistic fashion. For astrology to be true, I had to behave according to how I was defined in my own chart. Astrological expectations of myself and others became like iron masks, narrowing my field of vision, permitting only astrologically prescribed impressions to filter through.

One of the hardest things about coming out of the occult was recognizing and giving up these masks. For me, as an occultist, consciousness was All. Reality was purely a matter of what existed in my head. I was sure that if I changed my thoughts or consciousness, external reality would change accordingly. I honestly felt that if I stopped relating to people through their charts, everyone I knew would instantly become a stranger to me, and I would be a stranger to myself. I thought it would be like waking up from a pleasant dream into nightmarish reality. This was a gripping fear for three months as I struggled with the issue of what, if anything, I had to leave behind in order to commit my life to Jesus.

I had believed in the occult diagnosis of the human condition—all human problems stem from ignorance. I had taken the prescribed cure—a change in consciousness and an application of occult knowledge. I hoped in the occult prognosis—to become divine. Salvation, I believed, was by human effort through knowledge. Why wasn't it working?

THE TURNING POINT

Scripture starts with a different diagnosis. It says our dilemma is moral and relational springing from our rebellion and neutrality in relationship to God. Our problem is sin, inborn and freely chosen, which renders us incapable of relating to God and handicapped in relating to each other.

In addition, Scripture affirms that this problem of sin is beyond human ingenuity (Is 64:6; Jer 17:9; Rom 8:7, 8). It announces the fact that God has taken the initiative to deal with it on man's behalf. Salvation is by grace.

The solution God himself offers is moral and relational as opposed to mental and perceptual. God himself bears for us the just consequences of our hostility toward him in order to make possible a restored relationship with him (Is 53:5; Jn 3:16; 2 Cor 5:21).

My acceptance of what God has done on his own to address our corporate dilemma in general and mine in particular is called "faith." Since part of what, in faith, I accept, is the restoration of that which, by my sin, I broke, my faith implies a turning from sin, a repentance. What this faith allows grace to produce in me immediately and permanently is not a perceptual change, but a judicial one. My sin is no longer held against me in judgment. Furthermore, God's full restoration implies that I undergo a progressive character transformation. Conformity to the image of God's Son is a process of moral growth and character maturation.

When the spell of spiritual deception was broken in my life by the power of Jesus, the reality of my situation flooded in on me. For twelve years I had believed that all the universe was a single, divine reality, and that I, myself, was an evolving spark of that divinity. Distinctions between truth and falsehood, good and evil, were false dichotomies, illusions that I've made good progress in overcoming! My attitude toward morality was cynical: it was for those unevolved types who couldn't direct their own destinies.

Now suddenly, in a matter of moments, I could see the trickle-down effects of those false beliefs in my life. My relationships— friends, family, business, financial—were a web of deceit. Resentment and envy were growing wild behind a screen of self-righteousness. Immorality in my past had never been dealt with, only whitewashed and redefined. I was always my Number One. My own agenda was top priority at home and at work. I did whatever it took to get my way. I wasn't involved in any affairs, bank robberies, or ritual murders, but I suddenly realized I had no reason *not* to be, other than my own preference at the time.

It was conceivable that at some point my spiritual journey into divinity would require behavior that went against the grain of conventional morality. I felt certain that I would do whatever was necessary. There were no standards. That realization frightened me, especially as I began to see the deterioration in my life to that point.

"Sin" reentered my vocabulary, and I had to face the fact again that I was a creature, as powerless as I was rebellious. I'd had many engrossing spiritual experiences, but none had resulted in spiritual growth or life. I had to admit that my spiritual journey to that point had been a futile exercise in turning circles. I was no closer to the truth about anything, especially about myself as a human being and about God, than I had been twelve years before. In fact, I was more confused, and at the same time more certain that the only truth *was* confusion! Could all my twelve years of work, though, and devotion (the three yogic paths to the *achievement* of enlightenment) have been a spiritual placebo? All I had learned were more precise and refined methods for bringing out the worst in myself.

I knew I could no longer pretend to be my Creator. Nor could I restore myself to him, though I wanted to so much. There was something about knowing that I'd hit bottom that made me fear and long for holiness, for righteousness. Not to be "better than," not to be "righter than," but to be holy, to be righteous. I was finally at the point where I could never expect that of myself. I knew with a numb ache that it was outside my nature, beyond my reach. All I wanted then was to be in the shadow of the God who is holiness and righteousness, the God who is totally other: my Creator. It was only at this point that God could reach down to the bottom and dig me out and scrub me off and bring me home.

This is the turning point for all of us, including occultists: recognizing the hopelessness of reaching God through religious effort. The biblical diagnosis starts here. The biblical cure is God's offer to reach us, in spite of our condition, through his Son Jesus. If we take the cure, the prognosis is certain: immediate justification before God and gradual conformity to the image of God's Son. God has committed himself to see such people through this process of a moral growth and character development (Phil 1:6; 2:12b, 13).

The biblical prognosis is a fullness of individuality in a complete redemption: the assured attainment of perfect humanity (Rom 8:23). The occultist, in trying to overshoot this mark, suffers the loss of his individuality. He will never attain divinity, but by trying to become what he is not, his personal identity becomes more and more arbitrary to him. It recedes and becomes diffuse, mingling with the identities of other entities, persons, animals, and things he sees himself identical to. Limited, fulfillable personhood is sacrificed to an impersonal "higher consciousness" little by little in the daily routines of the occultist, and eventually perhaps leads to permanent possession.

SHARING JESUS WITH THE OCCULTIST

There are two things I share when I share Christ: the gospel and my faith. When I was in the occult, I knew a good number of Christians and attended church with my family on a regular basis. I never heard a clear presentation of the gospel. Ask your occultic friend: "Have you ever considered this: that Jesus Christ actually did die for our sins, just as the Old Testament foretold he would; that he actually was buried and he actually was raised on the third day, just like the Old Testament foretold he would be, and just as was reported by the eyewitnesses in the New Testament? Have you really considered that possibility?" Sharing Jesus through his Word is the most direct way we can help someone else get in touch with him.

At times there is an amazing readiness to turn to the Lord upon simply hearing the gospel, if the attitude of the messenger hasn't gotten in the way. More often, though, sharing the gospel becomes the focus for sharing our faith. Sharing our faith involves discussion of issues as well as the evidence of Jesus' authority and love in our lives. Here especially our attitude toward the person is important.

People and their ideas occur together in our experience, but each demands from us a different response. We are to avoid useless arguments in the spirit of love (2 Tm 2:23), yet contend for the faith (Jude 3). We must be sensitive and loving toward people while standing firm for the truth and even confronting that which opposes it. This isn't easy, but it is required.

We will have to address both people and their ideas. If we focus only on ideas, we may never reach the person. We may contend for the faith, but we will end up personally contentious as well. Whatever truth we can express will be debilitated by our detachment. It will seem more like arrogance.

On the other hand, if we focus only on the person, it isn't likely that he will hear from us anything that can set him free from his entrapment. We won't be likely to share the truth that hurts, let alone defend it, if it conflicts with our friend's own beliefs and ideas. Whatever love we can express while avoiding the risk that our friend may reject both truth and us will be debilitated by our own anxious need for approval.

Loving someone who rejects the truth, even truth that would save his life, surely does not require that I equivocate or reinterpret that truth to fit both of us. It is simply a more painful way of loving. Paul's advice to Timothy always applies (2 Tm 2:22-26). My attitude toward the person must be one of love and peace. I must avoid becoming ensnared in arguments and speculations which merely produce quarrels and so counteract the dynamics of evangelization. I must be kind, able to teach, and not resentful. When opposed, I must be able to gently guide and not react.

And I need to remember that no one comes to a knowledge of the truth about God directly from the lips of the person sharing the truth. That truth is always behind the door of repentance. It is a change of heart and a change of direction that leads us to a knowledge of the truth (2 Tm 2:25). It is a refusal of that change, a continuing to lead oneself on by all kinds of futile desires, that leads to the impotence of one who is "always learning, but never able to acknowledge the truth" (2 Tm 3:7). We need first and foremost to be in prayer for those with whom we share our faith, for the real work is done when God grants a change of heart.

NEEDS: WHO WILL MEET THEM?

What draws people into the occult? People are drawn in by their legitimate need to be in relationship to the supernatural. The problem is that they treat this relationship as one of identity with the supernatural in an effort to attain perfect human autonomy.[5]

During my own twelve years as an occultist, I felt three powerful needs related to the supernatural: a need for knowledge, a need for "initiation," and a need for power. My involvement in astrology and in other forms of divination, in channeling and past-life regression, in Eastern philosophies and in the ritual worship of the ascended masters was a full-scale attempt to meet these needs. And these needs were not felt only by me. They were shared by every occultist I knew.

The first is a need for supernatural knowledge. This legitimate need is distorted by fear and selfish desire into a counterfeit "need" for the biblically forbidden knowledge of other peoples' thoughts and intentions and of the future. Similarly, my arrogance distorted my legitimate need into a false need for access to *gnosis:* a supposedly special kind of knowledge restricted to an elite.

There are only certain kinds of non-ordinary knowledge which Scripture encourages us or allows us to seek in order to truly meet our need for such knowledge. The first is the knowledge of salvation, which is not hidden or restricted at all but revealed in God's Word. In fact, Jesus condemns those who attempt to hide or restrict it by obscuring the meaning of the Scriptures (Lk 11:52). Another special knowledge we are encouraged to seek is knowledge of God's will. But we seek this within the context of submission to him, which includes obedience to his commandments against occult activity, and by trusting him for wisdom and guidance (Prv 3:5, 6; Jer 33:3; Mt 7:8; Col 1:9; Jas 1:5).

My thirst for supernatural knowledge was also a need for meaning. I needed a framework in which to understand my interpersonal life and its ultimate purpose. The occult offered me metaphysical solutions to relational problems: knowledge of past lives, correction of energy imbalances, and realignment of personal and cosmic cycles. Love, I was led to believe, was an experiential state of harmony and unification that was attained through enlightened knowledge.

Scripture, on the other hand, defines my need for meaning in the interpersonal realm not as a need for mental acuity but as a need for moral clarity. It does not offer me metaphysical solutions as a result of occultic commitment, but promises me moral change as a result of commitment to Christ. Love is not the automatic result of knowledge (1 Cor 13:2; 8:1). It is rather an act of moral decision to the point of self-sacrifice (1 Jn 3:16; 4:10; Jn 15:13; 12:24; Lk 9:23, 24). My ultimate purpose as an occultist was cynical and nihilistic: to disappear into the All and Everything. Scripture tells me that my intended end and purpose is the maturity of my individual personhood in Christ (Eph 4:13), and the full attainment of a personal relationship with him as an end in itself (Phil 3:7, 8, 10, 11).

The second need I felt as an occultist was a need for "initiation." This is not so much a need for elitist status as for the opportunity to be given a new start, to be put on a new path, to turn my life around, to make a commitment. I thought "altered states of consciousness" would little by little renew my mind and the quality of my life. God's Word showed me that the need I felt for a new start was really my need for forgiveness and cleansing. What I was seeking in the commitment of initiation was the gift of regeneration.

Occultists are prepared for initiation in part through a series of subjective experiential changes in consciousness achieved in particular forms of meditation, occultic exercises, or drug use. The most basic result that I experienced in undergoing these changes was a rejection of the objective and external dimensions of reality and a devaluation of whatever needed to be expressed rationally and logically. I shared a contempt for language with the yogi, the mystic, and the Zen master. But here is how *God* prepares us to become regenerate: *through* his Word (1 Pt 1:23; Jas 1:18; Eph 5:26; Rom 10:14-17)! He is personal. He is a Speaker. He *intends* to be understood in his Word. He invites our response.

The third need which the occult addressed for me and for others is the need for power or "empowerment." But I learned from the Bible that God, too, seeks my empowerment (Eph 3:16, 18). The biblical word for it is "anointing," which is a special kind of empowerment based on God's sovereign choice. Occult empowerment is from the "divinity" of the self. Biblical empowerment is from the sovereign Creator God. Occultic technologies and pantheons of spiritual entities mediate power to me in the first case. It always seemed to me that what Christianity lacked was just such a systematic method for spiritual empowerment and growth, and of course a line of gurus to initiate and transmit that method to its serious adherents.

How *is* empowerment mediated in the Christian life? There are no magical methods or spiritual power-brokers. The anointing remains in me inasmuch as I remain in Jesus Christ (1 Jn 2:27). It is the technology of "abiding" (Jn 15:5). To remain or abide in Christ is for me to sustain a relationship with him, to participate in fellowship with him in his Word, in prayer, and in relationships with his people. Abiding implies as well that I live the rest of my life out of the power of this relationship.

The occultist comes to Christ through grace in repentant faith, just like everyone else does. But this process can be facilitated when the Christians he knows are modeling a life in which Christ meets the very needs he has in common with them.

WORKING THROUGH YOUR CHURCH

There are a great many things that local churches can do to evangelize people in the occult. None of them will get done by churches which are too complacent or disinterested to hammer out their own beliefs and convictions in the areas touched on in this chapter.

Some churches are characterized by the assumption that everyone who walks in the door shares the same beliefs, and that once they are assented to they need no further examination. Other churches see truth as largely relative and subjective, something which is created by human interaction rather than revealed by God and discovered by man. The first has no heart for God's truth; the second can't distinguish it from alternative ideas. The first is satisfied with parroting propositional truths; the second can't tolerate prepositional truths. Neither can be used to help someone out of the pit of destructive spiritual deception.

The first thing the local church can do is encourage the corporate examination of belief in an atmosphere of acceptance. People should be encouraged to examine their doubts as well, rather than hide them and hope they go away. Church members should search the Scriptures together to grow in the truth, examining their personal beliefs in its light.

On a practical level, the local church can reach out with compassion to those coming out of the occult. In many cases, especially where there has been cultic involvement, ritual abuse, or isolation within the occult, there may be serious psychological damage or the person's life may be in danger. These people often need a transition time and place. The local church, especially in conjunction with countercult ministries, could work toward the provision of "safe houses" and provide funds to help those coming out of the occult.

Integration of former occultists within the local church may at times need special attention. At the very least, it is necessary to encourage these new Christians in the study of God's Word within a suitable small group setting. Special attention needs to be paid to the growth in their understanding of their relationship to God and the supernatural. Prayer partners are especially important, not only for modeling but also for accountability and help in the spiritual warfare which these new Christians inevitably face. In extreme cases, where the culture of the church is just too alien from the cultural-religious experience of the person coming out, there may have to be a "transitional church." This is essentially a small group, two to four, from the local church, who meet with the person regularly to share the Word, pray, and have fellowship in a more informal and less threatening atmosphere.

Additionally, it would be helpful to have within the local body a person designated to coordinate activities pertaining to apologetics. This would take apologetics out of the library stacks and put it into the street where it belongs in our post-biblical culture. Apologetics activities would be functions of either evangelism or discipleship, but would focus on building up a self-conscious, articulate faith in the members, and training them to share that faith effectively. Willow Creek Community Church in South Barrington, Illinois, has pioneered the development of this concept.[6] It and a number of churches modeled after its philosophy of ministry have set an excellent pattern for practical apologetics.

The training of a core group within the local church would enable that body to reach out effectively to occultists and other specific groups in many ways. The body could send teams *out* of the church to generate public meetings or seminars that address spiritual issues on neutral turf. Specific occult ideas and practices could be addressed in this way within a format of debate or general critique. Certain issues in supernaturalism such as miracles, angels, and man's spiritual powers provide an attractive focus for a comparison of worldviews.

Team members could attend occultic events and seminars and add interest by asking informed questions that may put a hole or two in the occultic worldview. The idea is that the local church get the gospel out into the marketplace of ideas and be ready to answer questions (1 Pt 3:15). A friend once said that Mars Hill, of Acts 17:22, was the Phil Donahue Show of Paul's time. We would do well to follow the pattern set by Paul in Acts 17 for approaching those of an alien worldview with the gospel.

SPIRITUAL WARFARE

Wherever there is an effort to share with the captives the truth that will make them free, there is spiritual warfare. An assault on the occult is an assault on the "god of this age," and he doesn't let his subjects go easily. Any work to counteract occultic influence needs to be fortified by consistent prayer. Two key principles of our warfare praying should inform our actions and our ministry with courage and boldness. First, we stand in and work out of the authority of Jesus Christ when we engage in spiritual warfare. God raised Jesus from the dead and seated him at his right hand far above all "rule and authority, power and dominion" (Eph 1:20, 21). Then he "raised us up with Christ and seated us with him" (Eph 2:6), that is, "far above all rule and authority, power and dominion." It is from this position of victory and authority that we are enjoined to struggle "not against flesh and blood, but against the rulers, against the authorities, against the powers of this dark world and against the spiritual forces of evil in the heavenly realms" (Eph 6:12).

When an occultist comes to Christ, he does not need to be convinced that these powers of evil are personal, supernatural entities. The issues involved in their identification are dealt with excellently in D.A. Carson's *Biblical Interpretation and the Church.* Carson makes the point that the powers themselves are personal agencies which use impersonal structures and traditions to mediate their personal intentions of the deception of human beings.[7] In Christ, our authority is over these supernatural entities who have insinuated themselves into the structures and traditions of our cultures. Our authority in Christ is based on his finished work. "He disarmed the powers and authorities, he made a public spectacle of them, triumphing over them by the cross" (Col 2:15). We stand in Christ at the end of history, already victorious. We stand there by faith, not by sight.

The second principle of spiritual warfare we need to implement is the principle of using that authority to claim back God's own. From our position in Christ and in his name, we stand firm in prayer, claiming back all of the person, issue by issue, for the God who created and redeemed him. We are the agents of reconciliation of the living Christ who liberates from bondage. We are engaged in battle against real spiritual agencies. We are in a real sense bringing back home prisoners of war. They depend on our determination and ingenuity to seek them out. They need our compassion and our patience to win them over. And then they need faithful prayer partners and intercessors to claim with them in Christ their complete deliverance from the power of Satan into the hand of their heavenly Father.

SEVEN

Jehovah's Witnesses

Robert Passantino

- "... we should be working under the direction of the Governing Body and the older men in our congregations.... And if one of those instructions were for us to jump, our only response should be 'How high?' and 'How far?'"[1]

- "Jehovah is using only one organization today to accomplish his will. To receive everlasting life in the earthly Paradise we must identify that organization and serve God as part of it."[2]

- "... come to Jehovah's organization for salvation."[3]

- "Jehovah God has also provided his visible organization.... Unless we are in touch with this channel of communication that God is using, we will not progress along the road of life, no matter how much Bible reading we do."[4]

- "Avoid independent thinking... questioning the counsel that is provided by God's visible organization."[5]

BIBLE READING IS OUT. Blind submission is in. The Watchtower Bible and Tract Society, more commonly known as the Jehovah's Witnesses, has spoken. God's organization today, his mouthpiece, opposes "Christendom," which erroneously encourages Bible study, personal responsibility before God, and the indwelling, sanctifying presence of the Holy Spirit. That's what the Watchtower Society wants us to believe, anyway. The Watchtower leadership, called the Governing Body, rules with an iron fist over more than 3.6 million members in two hundred twelve countries.[6] Since there are more than three quarters of a million Jehovah's Witnesses in the United States alone,[7] your chances of encountering a zealous Watchtower door-to-door missionary are high. Where did this monolithic organization come from? Why would anyone submit blindly to such a religious autocracy? What do Jehovah's Witnesses believe that sets them in opposition to Evangelical Christianity?

HISTORY

The Jehovah's Witnesses have their roots in a small Bible study, formed in 1872, led by Charles Taze Russell, a man with no formal religious training. Russell had been raised a Congregationalist, but rejected orthodoxy because of his aversion to the doctrine of eternal punishment. He also abandoned orthodoxy's doctrines of the Trinity, the deity of Christ, and salvation by grace alone.

Russell was born in Allegheny, Pennsylvania, in 1852. He started his Bible study when he was only twenty years old. He taught that the "truths" he shared with the study members had been lost or abandoned by the historic church, but he had discovered them through his careful, inspired Bible study. One of the older Watchtower publications equates Russell's work, and that of his successor, J.F. Rutherford, with the very work of Jesus Christ, the prophets, and the apostles:

True, in recent times men such as C.T. Russell and J.F. Rutherford participated prominently in this world-wide work as Jehovah's witnesses,[8] even as in ancient days Christ Jesus, Paul, Peter, John the Baptist, Moses, Abraham, Noah, Abel, and many others participated prominently in the work as Jehovah's witnesses.[9]

Russell joined another aberrant Bible teacher, N.H. Barbour, in 1879, and the two published a magazine, *The Herald of the Morning,* which was gradually transformed over the years after Russell split with Barbour until today it is published as *The Watchtower*. In 1884, after the break with Barbour, Russell and his followers formed Zion's Watch Tower Tract Society, today officially called the Watchtower Bible and Tract Society. Russell's followers grew in number, largely through his retitled magazine, then called *Zion's Watch Tower*, and his public speaking. Russell, called "Pastor" by his followers, wrote a series of seven doctrinal books, first called *The Millennial Dawn* and later titled *The Studies in the Scriptures*.[10] Hints of the increasingly authoritarian stance of the Society abound in Russell's writings. He declared that studying his books brought more spiritual light to the reader than reading the Bible itself!

> Not only do we find that people cannot see the divine plan in studying the Bible by itself, but we see, also, that if anyone lays the "Scripture Studies" aside, even after he has used them, after he has become familiar with them, after he has read them for ten years—if he then lays them aside and ignores them and goes to the Bible alone, though he has understood his Bible for ten years, our experience shows that within two years he goes into darkness.[11]

Despite later Watchtower claims to the contrary, Russell's teachings are the basis for Watchtower theology today. The Watchtower is in a dilemma: it accuses Christendom of elevating individual men to positions of authority, and yet it owes its fundamental structure and teachings to one man, Charles Taze Russell. The solution? Deny Russell's essential importance, but use his contributions anyway. Russell denied the Trinity, the deity of Christ, the bodily resurrection of Christ, the deity and personality of the Holy Spirit, the existence of hell, and the consciousness of man after death. Russell also taught that other religions and members of Christendom were in darkness, doomed to extinction, while only followers of his teachings were in the truth. Today's Watchtower is doctrinally identical.

Russell was succeeded at his death in 1916 by J.F. Rutherford, who gave the common name "Jehovah's Witnesses," to followers in 1931. He continued in Russell's teachings and solidified the organizational aspects of the Society. He was in turn succeeded at his death in 1942 by Nathan Homer Knorr, under whose leadership the

Governing Body became the ultimate authority rather than an individual man. At Knorr's death in 1977, leadership was assumed by Frederick W. Franz. Because of the well-oiled machinery of the Governing Body, Franz has been able to remain at the helm despite his advancing years (he was born in 1893) and increasingly limited personal participation.

Today Jehovah's Witnesses around the world march in step. They distribute the same literature, teach the same book studies, and hold identical weekly congregation meetings and annual regional conferences around the world. The Witness who dissents is cut off, forced to leave the congregation, and shunned not only by his congregation, but also by his Witness friends and even close family members. The only reason Witnesses can boast of internal unity is because there is absolutely no toleration of differences of opinion or independent thinking.

DOCTRINE

Jehovah's Witnesses are perhaps best known for their restricted lifestyles, including the Watchtower bans on celebrating birthdays and holidays, accepting blood transfusions, serving in the armed forces, and voting. Strict compliance with time quotas for volunteer door-to-door witnessing accounts for their visible presence in most American neighborhoods, even though their American membership is less than one million. The focus of the door-to-door encounters is usually the imminent Battle of Armageddon, at which time all but the faithful Witnesses will be destroyed.

How soon is this Battle? Throughout its history, the Watchtower Society has attempted to answer that question, first with Russell's "prophecies," then, after his death, with their own.[12] So far, they've never been right. A quick perusal of their membership history shows, however, that prophesying the near end of the world is a good recruitment technique, even though there is a sharp drop in commitment immediately after the prophecy fails. The false prophecies of the Watchtower are hard for the Society to explain, although it has certainly made a gallant effort. Within the last fifteen years it has offered such explanations as 1. as the light of biblical interpretation gets brighter, we get more accurate; 2. we may have claimed to be prophets, but never *inspired* prophets; 3. just like a sailboat has to tack into the wind to leave a harbor, so we sometimes "tack" in our teachings—we *look* like we're going the wrong way, but eventually we'll get out of the harbor; and, the most recent, 4. better to be over-eager than unprepared:

It is easy for the established churches of Christendom and other people to criticize Jehovah's Witnesses because their publications have, at times, stated that certain things could take place on certain dates. But is not such line of action in harmony with Christ's injunction to "keep on the watch"? Is it not far preferable to make some mistakes because of over eagerness to see God's purposes accomplished . . . ?[13]

The Bible's evaluation of false prophecy is, however, much simpler. Deuteronomy gives us two very simple tests of a prophet. Deuteronomy 18:21, 22 declares that a prophet's prophecy must come to pass:

You may say to yourselves, "How can we know when a message has not been spoken by the Lord?" If what a prophet proclaims in the name of the Lord does not take place or come true, that is a message the Lord has not spoken. That prophet has spoken presumptuously. Do not be afraid of him.[14]

Deuteronomy 13:1-3 further demands that a prophet's words, even if they come to pass, must glorify the true God, or else the prophet is false:

If a prophet, or one who foretells by dreams, appears among you and announces a miraculous sign or wonder, and if the sign or wonder of which he has spoken takes place, and he says, "Let us follow other gods" (gods you have not known) "and let us worship them," you must not listen to the words of that prophet or that prophet or dreamer . . .

Jehovah's Witnesses fail the biblical test of prophecy not only because they have failed to prophesy accurately, but because they deny the biblical God and the clear teachings of his Word.

DOCTRINAL EVALUATION

Watchtower doctrine deviates from Scripture in two general categories. The first needs only a cursory examination and concerns peripheral, or secondary, doctrine. Such doctrinal deviations do not in themselves separate one from salvation (although the Watchtower teaches that Witnesses who disagree with them in these areas are destined for extinction). Most of the Witness lifestyle restrictions fall into this category. The Witnesses are taught that the bans on holidays, transfusions, and government participation are mandated by Scripture.[15]

The mandatory door-to-door witnessing derives from a Watchtower misunderstanding of Acts 20:20, where Paul said, "I did not hold back from telling you any of the things that were profitable nor from teaching you publicly and from house to house."[16] Witnesses are taught that door-to-door witnessing is one of the marks of God's true church. In fact, Witnesses are taught that their door-to-door work is helping Jehovah to "mark" the righteous from the unrighteous preparatory to God's judgment at the Battle of Armageddon. It is explained in a Watchtower publication specifically designed as a handbook reference for door-to-door workers. Here is what the Witness is supposed to answer to a householder's question about why he is going door-to-door:

Have you ever wondered why people like me volunteer to make these calls even though we know that the majority of householders may not welcome us? (Give the gist of Matthew 25:31-33, explaining that a separating of people of all nations is taking place and that their response to the Kingdom message is an important factor in this. Or state the gist of Ezekiel 9:1-11, explaining that, on the basis of people's reaction to the Kingdom message, everyone is being "marked" either for preservation through the great tribulation or for destruction by God.)[17]

Unfortunately for the average Witness, no matter how God intends to separate the righteous from the unrighteous, that judgment is on the basis of one's allegiance to the true God of the Bible, through the power of the Holy Spirit and because of Christ's atoning work on the cross, not because one witnesses door-to-door or doesn't salute the flag. Not only is the Watchtower Society wrong about these peripheral issues, it is also wrong about the essentials of biblical faith.

THE TRINITY

Jehovah's Witnesses deny the doctrine of the Trinity. They believe that only the Father is God, and that his name is Jehovah. He created Jesus Christ as Michael the Archangel. The Holy Spirit is God's active force, not personal, and not God.

> The evidence is indisputable that the dogma of the Trinity is not found in the Bible, nor is it in harmony with what the Bible teaches. . . . It grossly misrepresents the true God.[18]

The Watchtower has distorted the Christian doctrine of the Trinity so that what appears to be scriptural refutation of it is persuasive. Jehovah's Witnesses think that the Trinity is illogical and contradictory, *e.g.*, that belief in the Trinity is a belief that one god can be three gods. Witnesses think trinitarians confuse the persons of the Godhead, believing that the Father *is* the Son.[19]

However, the Christian doctrine of the Trinity is not accurately portrayed by the Watchtower Society. The Trinity is a widely used theological term that accurately describes the biblical teaching concerning the tripersonal nature of God. The Bible teaches that within the nature of the one true God (Is 42:8; 43:10; 44:6, 8; 45:21; 1 Cor 8:4-6; Neh 9:6; 1 Tm 2:5) there are three eternal, distinct, divine Persons (Mt 28:19; Lk 3:21, 22): the Father (2 Pt 1:17); the Son (Word) (Jn 1:1-3, 14; 8:24, 58; Col 1:15-19; Ti 2:13); and the Holy Spirit (Acts 13:2; 10:19, 20; Heb 3:7-11; Acts 5:3, 4; Heb 9:14).

The doctrine of the Trinity is biblical. It is neither illogical nor unreasonable, but its *complete* comprehension is beyond our finite logic and reason.[20] We do not irrationally say that we believe in three gods and one god, or in three persons and one person, but we do logically say that the Bible teaches one true God in three divine Persons.[21]

JESUS CHRIST

According to the Watchtower Society, Jesus Christ is not the only true God, the almighty, Jehovah. He is instead the first and mightiest creation of Jehovah God, created as Michael the Archangel, and by whom everything *else* was created. Michael voluntarily gave up his existence as a spirit creature, and was recreated from Jehovah's memory as a man, Jesus, the Second Adam, whose life and death provided escape from Adam's original sin. He was a perfect "ransom sacrifice." That is, he bought back exactly what Adam lost, no more and no less. Because of Jehovah's "unmerited favor" (grace) in providing Jesus, faithful followers can obtain approval from God by obedience to his commandments and affiliation with his organization.

Definition: The only-begotten Son of God, the only Son produced by Jehovah alone. This Son is the firstborn of all creation. By means of him all other things in heaven and on earth were created. He is the second-greatest personage in the universe. It is this Son whom Jehovah sent to the earth to give his life as a ransom for mankind, thus opening the way to eternal life for those of Adam's offspring who would exercise faith. . . .[22]

Jehovah's Witnesses are taught that to believe Jesus is God is to believe in two gods, the Father and Jesus. They accuse Christians of being polytheistic, that is, of believing in more than one god. However, not only is this a misunderstanding of the Christian doctrine of the Trinity, but it is also anomalous to their own insistence that Jesus is a "mighty" god, but not the "almighty" God, Jehovah. The Watchtower translation of John 1:1 bears out this inconsistency:

"In [the] beginning the Word was, and the Word was with God, and the Word was a god."[23] Extensive research and writing has been done refuting the mistranslations and misinterpretations of the Watchtower in this and other passages, including cogent New Testament Greek arguments by premier Greek scholars such as Dr. Julius R. Mantey.[24] However, the context of the passage itself mitigates against the New World Translation. Here is the verse, in context:

In the beginning was the Word, and the Word was with God, and the Word was God. He was with God in the beginning. Through him all things were made; without him nothing was made that has been made. Jn 1:1-3

The New World Translation, in contrast to The New King James Version above, or any reputable translation, opposes the clear Bible teaching that there is only one true God (Is 43:10; 44:8; Jn 17:3; Dt 32:39). How could God emphatically state in these verses that there are no created gods, and that there is no god with him, and yet say, by inspiration through the monotheist John to his monotheistic Jewish audience, according to Jehovah's Witnesses, that "in the beginning" there was "a god" with him? The Jehovah's Witnesses become polytheists rather than the Christians. Any attempt to redefine the term "god" to harmonize their view is futile.

John 1:3 clearly states that the Word (Jesus) is the Creator of all things. In fact, John has emphasized this fact as much as he possibly can by stating it both positively ("all things were made through him") and negatively ("without him nothing was made that was made"). This literary device, called antithetical parallelism, is a strong, all-inclusive way to state that Jesus is the Creator.

If we divide all existing entities into two classes, what has been made and what has not been made, to which class would the Word of John 1:1-3 belong? Created or uncreated? Obviously, he would belong to the class of what has not been made, what is uncreated. This directly contradicts the Watchtower translation and interpretation of John 1:1, but harmonizes exactly with the biblical doctrine of the Trinity and with verses such as Isaiah 44:24, where Jehovah declares, "I am the Lord who makes all things, who stretches out the heavens all alone, who spreads abroad the earth by myself."

The Jehovah's Witnesses have only a few verses they have been taught to misconstrue in their attempt to support their teaching that Jesus is created. One example will show the inadequacies of their attempts.

The definition of Jesus Christ quoted above from the Watchtower includes the phrase "This Son is the firstborn of all creation." The phrase is adapted from Colossians 1:15, and the Jehovah's Witness interprets "firstborn" to mean "first-created." Witnesses are taught that Jesus is the first-created, created before the rest of creation. However, that is not the meaning of Paul's usage of firstborn in Colossians. Leaving aside technical Greek arguments,[25] the context of the passage itself denies the definition "first-created":

He is the image of the invisible God, the firstborn over all creation. For by him all things were created that are in heaven and that are on earth, visible and invisible, whether thrones or dominions or principalities or powers. All things were created through him and for him. And he is before all things, and in him all things consist. And he is the head of the body, the church, who is the beginning, the firstborn from the dead, that in all things he may have the preeminence. Col 1:15-18

Can Jesus be the first-created if all things are created through him and for him, and if he is before all things? Of course not! No wonder, then, that the New World Translation changes the passage: "because by means of him all [other][26] things. . . . All [other] things have been created through him. . . . Also, he is before all [other] things and by means of him all [other] things were made to exist. . . ." The word "other" is inserted four times, totally without warrant in the Greek or the context, in a futile attempt to reconcile Christ's creative preeminence with Watchtower theology. However, further insurmountable problems arise from the Watchtower interpretation of firstborn as first-created.

The word firstborn is used in the same context in referring to Christ as "the firstborn from the dead." Christ is not literally raised first, since there were people raised from the dead before him in both the Old and New Testaments. Firstborn cannot mean first-one-born from the dead in verse 18. It means, instead, that he was the one raised with power and authority over death—or, as verse 18 concludes, "that in all things he may have the preeminence." Preeminence is exactly the meaning of firstborn in verse 15, the "firstborn over all creation" is the one with the preeminence, or the right to rule, over creation. Verse 16 bears this out, completing the thought by beginning with "for" or "because." Why is he the firstborn, the preeminent one, over all creation? Because he created everything, and everything was created for him. This interpretation of firstborn fits the Greek usage, the biblical usage,[27] Paul's use of the term in verse 18, and the immediate context of verse 16.

The Watchtower translation and interpretation, on the other hand, violates the Greek, biblical, and Pauline usage of the term, and the context of verse 16. Jesus is not first-created, and such an interpretation of firstborn makes the *because* of verse 16 nonsense. His own action (creative) after he supposedly began to exist could not have *caused* his existence. One is not created because he creates other things. If such were the case, then the Watchtower's Jehovah would have to be created because *he* created a thing (Jesus).

Another area in which Witnesses have been confused concerning the deity of Christ is that of his incarnation. Witnesses think Christians are illogical for believing that Christ is God and man. God is eternal, man is created; therefore, they reason, Christ can't possibly be created and uncreated at the same time. What they fail to understand is that Christ, the eternal second person of the Trinity, never ceased being God, but took on an additional nature, that of a human being, in the incarnation.[28] Philippians 2:1-11 expresses this clearly. As is true with most Witness misunderstandings, a look at the context clarifies Christian teaching and refutes the Watchtower interpretation. The passage reads:

> If you have any encouragement from being united with Christ, if any comfort from his love, if any fellowship with the Spirit, if any tenderness and compassion, then make my joy complete by being like-minded, having the same love, being one in spirit and purpose. Do nothing out of selfish ambition or vain conceit, but in humility consider others better than yourselves. Each of you should look not only to your own interests, but also to the interests of others.
>
> Your attitude should be the same as that of Christ Jesus:
>
> Who, being in very nature God, did not consider equality with God something to be grasped, but made himself nothing, taking the very nature of a servant, being made in human likeness. And being found in appearance as a man, he humbled himself and became obedient to death—even death on a cross! Phil 2:1-8

The Watchtower interprets this passage to mean that Christ, ever aware that he was *not* almighty God, had a "form" of God in that he was a spirit creature before he became a man, but that he would never dare even to think that he could "seize" Godhood from the Father. Instead, he humbly surrendered his life to be a ransom sacrifice on our behalf.

The context of the passage contradicts this interpretation. The theme of Philippians 2:1-11 is humility. Paul admonishes the Philippian Christians to be humble toward one another, even to the point of acting *as though* their brothers and sisters were better than themselves. After all, says Paul, consider the premier example of humility, Jesus Christ. Jesus Christ, although he was exactly equal to the Father as to his divine nature, humbled himself to the Father's will. In the same way, although he was exactly equal to any other man as to his human nature, he humbled himself to all humanity by enduring the cross on our behalf. It is not humility to submit to one to whom you are intrinsically inferior. It is simple acknowledgement of fact. True humility comes from a voluntary submission based on intrinsic equality. Just as "form of a servant" means that Christ truly was a servant, so "form of God" means that Christ truly is God. The two parallels, one of humility, that is, between Christians and Jesus; and the other of form, that is, between Christ's deity and humanity, are undeniable. Far from denying the deity of Christ, Philippians 2:1-11 clearly affirms the absolute deity of Christ, our supreme example of humility in the face of equality.

Our final evaluation of the Watchtower teaching about Jesus Christ is its denial of the bodily resurrection. The Watchtower states, "The firstborn one from the dead was not raised out of the grave a human creature, but he was raised a spirit."[29] Concerning its reasoning for this denial of his resurrection it says, ". . . if, when he was resurrected, Jesus had taken back his human body of flesh and blood, which had been given in sacrifice to pay the ransom price, what effect would that have had on the provision he was making to relieve faithful persons of the debt of sin?"[30]

In fact, the Watchtower teaches that the person ceases to exist at his physical death: "For [bodily resurrection] to be possible, of course, humans would have to have an immaterial soul that could separate from the physical body. The Bible does not teach such a thing."[31] Instead, the Watchtower teaches that Jehovah re-created the spirit being who had once been Michael the Archangel; had ceased being Michael to become Jesus, only a man; and who then forever surrendered his human existence on the cross. This re-creation "involves a reactivating of the life pattern of the individual, which life pattern God has retained in his memory."[32]

Contrary to Watchtower teaching, Jesus Christ was raised, victorious over death, in the same material body in which he had died, but now glorified and resurrected. In Luke 24:39 Jesus expressly denies that he is a "spirit creature" by saying, "a spirit does not have flesh and bones as you see I have." In John 2:19-21, Jesus specifically prophesies the nature of his resurrection by saying:

> Jesus answered them, "Destroy this temple, and I will raise it again in three days." The Jews replied, "It has taken forty-six years to build this temple, and you are going to raise it in three days?" But the temple he had spoken of was his body. After he was raised from the dead, his disciples recalled what he had said. Then they believed the Scripture and the words that Jesus had spoken.

Finally, in John 20:24-29 we find Jesus complying with Thomas' test to prove the resurrection: he must touch the same scarred body with his own hands. Thomas' response carries the conviction of Christ's preeminence over death and his absolute deity: "My Lord and my God!"

The Watchtower response to these verses? "Jesus evidently materialized bodies on these occasions as angels had done in the past when appearing to humans.... to strengthen the conviction of the disciples that Jesus had actually been raised."[33] This makes no sense if his resurrection was not supposed to be bodily. Why would a physical body be proof of a predicted *immaterial* resurrection? It wouldn't. Instead, it would make Jesus a deliberate deceiver, who indulged his disciples' wrong idea of a material body proving an immaterial resurrection. The Watchtower's teachings cannot be reconciled to Scripture.

SALVATION

The Watchtower misunderstanding of biblical salvation follows from its misunderstanding of the atonement, Christ's sacrifice on the cross. With the Witnesses' presupposition that Christ's was an exactly equal ransom sacrifice to Adam's original sin, it is no wonder that Watchtower salvation becomes grace *plus* obedience. Christ may atone for Adam's sin, but the individual is stuck with the burden of his own sins. This chapter opened with some shocking quotes from Watchtower literature concerning the supreme authority of the organization. The clear teaching is to "come to Jehovah's organization for salvation" and "unless we are in touch with this channel of communication that God is using, we will not progress along the road to life, no matter how much Bible reading we do."

The effect of this teaching on the average Jehovah's Witness is that, while he believes Jesus' death has provided the *opportunity* to merit God's favor and be sanctified, he feels compelled to work for Jehovah's approval. This combination of faith and works denies the clear biblical teaching of salvation by grace alone as expressed in such verses as Ephesians 2:8-10; Romans 4:1-8; Galatians 5:1-6; and Philippians 3:1-9. Hebrews 7:26-28 explains the superiority of Christ's human and divine sacrifice:

Such a High Priest meets our need—one who is holy, blameless, pure, set apart from sinners, exalted above the heavens. Unlike the other high priests, he does not need to offer up sacrifices day after day, first for his own sins, and then for the sins of the people. He sacrificed for their sins once for all when he offered himself. For the law appoints as high priests men who are weak; but the oath, which came after the law, appointed the Son, who has been perfected forever.

The Watchtower doctrines contradict clear biblical revelation and the most essential doctrines of the historic Christian church. Jesus declared, "if you do not believe that I am, you will die in your sins."[34]

EVANGELIZING JEHOVAH'S WITNESSES

If we believe Jesus' words in John 8:24, then we must commit ourselves to evangelizing Jehovah's Witnesses, who have been sold a wrong Jesus, a wrong gospel, and a wrong spirit (2 Cor 11:4). The way we evangelize must conform to the directives of Scripture, outlined in 2 Timothy 2:24-26:

> And the Lord's servant must not quarrel; instead, he must be kind to everyone, able to teach, not resentful. Those who oppose him he must gently instruct, in the hope that God will grant them repentance leading them to a knowledge of the truth, and that they will come to their senses and escape from the trap of the devil, who has taken them captive to do his will.

The best evangelism is biblical evangelism, and this passage gives the elements for a successful witnessing encounter with a Jehovah's Witness (or any other nonbeliever).

First, emotional outbursts and anger never win anyone to Christ. Paul says we are not to quarrel, but *be gentle*. If you have done your homework, know your subject, and pray before your encounter, you should be able to keep to the subject matter without being drawn into the Witness's sometimes hostile arguments.

Second, we must *be able to teach*. That means that we know God's Word, we know what we believe as Christians, and we have given careful thought to the clarity and logic of our presentation.[35] Paul continues in Timothy to affirm the importance of studying Scripture:

> But as for you, continue in what you have learned and have become convinced of, because you know those from whom you have learned it, and how from infancy you have known the holy Scriptures, which are able to make you wise for salvation through faith in Christ Jesus. All Scripture is god-breathed and is useful for teaching, for rebuking, correcting and training in righteousness, so that the man of God may be thoroughly equipped for every good work. 2 Tm 3:14-17

You do not need to be a Greek or Hebrew scholar, or a logician, in order to explain biblical truth to a Jehovah's Witness. But you do need to know the teachings of God's Word and how to present them persuasively to the Witness.

Third, we are to *be patient*. In the last seventeen years of my ministry I have talked to literally thousands of non-believers. Each of those who have become Christians did so after they had had several encounters with one or more Christians. We cannot force anyone to become a Christian, and our patience should be our ally in persuading the Witness to examine the evidence carefully, to check out what we are saying, and to make a careful assessment of the discrepancies between what he has been taught and what the Scriptures actually say.

Fourth, we are to *be humble* when we correct those in opposition. It may be obvious to us, for example, that John 20:28 affirms the absolute deity of Christ, but it might not be obvious at all to someone blinded by false teaching. Remember, each of us was spiritually ignorant before we were saved—we "once walked according to the course of this world, according to the prince of the power of the air, the spirit who now works in the sons of disobedience" (Eph 2:2). Earlier I discussed Philippians 2:1-11, and its theme of humility, exemplified by Jesus Christ. If God the Son could humble himself to the cross on behalf of us sinners, it shouldn't be hard to treat nonbelievers as we would like to be treated.

FOLLOW THE GOLDEN RULE

I call this the "Golden Rule Apologetic." Don't press the Witness harder than you want to be pressed. Don't ridicule him for his belief if you wouldn't like to be ridiculed for being a Christian. If you want the Witness to understand when you don't have an answer and need time to research it, then give the Witness the same opportunity to try to defend his belief. This does not mean that all religious views are of the same value, or are only relatively true. But it means that the God of truth, in whose name we evangelize, doesn't need us to bully, intellectually twist, psychologically manipulate, or emotionally exploit nonbelievers in order to win. If you follow the Golden Rule Apologetic, you will establish fair, objective standards of argumentation and biblical interpretation by which the truth will be manifested.

For example, if you accuse your Witness friend of being a victim of mind control, what criteria do you use? Be sure your list of characteristics couldn't be misconstrued to condemn Christianity as a mind control cult. Some critics fail to understand Christianity's worldview and wrongly lump Christianity with the cults. They might say, Christianity teaches exclusivism, absolute allegiance, even above that to one's family (Mt 10:35-37); dissociation with the world (Is 52:11); and abandonment of relationships with non-believers (2 Cor 6:15). Use the Golden Rule Apologetic and don't unfairly categorize the cultist you are evangelizing.[36]

Here's an example of how using the Golden Rule Apologetic helps in explaining the reasonable force of an argument. Let's say you are arguing for the personality of the Holy Spirit with a Jehovah's Witness. Every time you point to a verse ascribing personal attributes to the Holy Spirit, the Witness tries to explain it away by saying the language is figurative, personification, or some other literary figure of speech not meant to be taken literally. Apply the Golden Rule. Ask the Witness why he believes that Satan, who does not have a body, is a person. He'll point to verses ascribing personal attributes such as intelligence, the ability to communicate, will, capability for interpersonal relationship, etc., to Satan. But wait, you respond, how come when we're talking about the Holy Spirit these same attributes can be explained away, but when it comes to Satan, they prove he's a person? You have shown the Witness that if he is objective, he must either give up the personality of Satan (which you both agree would not be biblical), or accept the personality of the Holy Spirit, the first step in proving the personality and deity of the Holy Spirit.

Fifth, 2 Timothy 2:24-26 reminds us that the fruit of our evangelism can come only through *the intervening power of God* granting them repentance, enlightening them to the truth, and releasing them from the bondage of the devil. Spiritual bondage is broken by spiritual power, not academic, intellectual, psychological, or emotional power. I don't mean that there is no place for apologetics,[37] biblical counseling, or a demonstration of personal commitment in love. In fact, all are aspects of our biblical obligation toward others.[38] But one can only come to salvation by the direct guidance of the Holy Spirit to repentance and trust in Christ's atoning death on the cross. This principle is often ignored or forgotten by those who witness to cultists.

For example, sometimes I get frustrated when I'm evangelizing a cultist and he doesn't believe what seems to me to be a simple statement of fact. I amass more facts, more documentation, and more scholarship, thinking that if he sees the academic soundness of Christianity, he will turn from his ignorance. Other times I can't understand why the cultist I'm talking with doesn't see the logic of what I consider to be a very clear argument. I try to explain it two, three, four different ways, thinking that if I can find the right intellectual argument, the light will dawn and the cultist will repent. Then I remember, "God perhaps will grant him or her repentance."

CONCLUSION

The principles of 2 Timothy 2:24-26 provide a biblical foundation for evangelizing Jehovah's Witnesses. Combine this biblical foundation with a commitment to the essentials of biblical faith (the doctrines of the Trinity, Jesus Christ, and salvation), and with a compassionate, accurate understanding of the worldview the Witness has embraced. You will be equipped for successful evangelism of Jehovah's Witnesses.

My wife and I once shared the gospel with a roomful of Jehovah's Witnesses, some of whom were in positions of congregational leadership. We spent hours talking about the Watchtower, the doctrine of the Trinity, the deity and resurrection of Christ, and biblical salvation. None of the Witnesses seemed to be affected at all. On the way home, my wife and I were discouraged. Nothing had seemed to penetrate the Watchtower mentality.

The next morning, one of the Witness couples called us. They told us, "When you were talking last night, it was like bright sunshine filled the room. The Jesus you talked about is the Jesus we really believe in. We were tricked by the Watchtower, but now, no matter what, we have to follow the Jesus God showed us last night through what you said." Why did those two come to salvation, but not any of the other Witnesses who had been there? I know it didn't depend on our intellect, academics, or communicative skills: "It does not, therefore, depend on man's desire or effort, but on God's mercy" (Rom 9:16); and "so neither he who plants nor he who waters is anything, but only God, who makes things grow." (1 Cor 3:7).

EIGHT

The Unity School of Christianity

Kurt Van Gorden

S EVERAL YEARS AGO I went into the office complex of a large Christian church in California to see the pastor. This church has several thousand members and is known for its ministries worldwide. While I was waiting for my appointment, I began to shuffle through the magazine collection on the end table. To my surprise I found a copy of *Unity* magazine and *Daily Word*, published by the Unity School of Christianity in Unity Village, Missouri.

This was not the first time that I have seen *Unity* in the magazine collections at Christian churches and in Christian businesses. All too often some devoted Unity follower will buy a subscription for the church or business. Those in the office rarely take the time to read the material on the inside. As a result, their offices become promoters of the Unity worldview.

I have known two pastors from California who have quit their pulpit ministries to become Unity teachers. A Methodist writer on world religions, Marcus Bach, wrote *The Unity Way of Life*, which gives the picture of Unity as the only viable answer for Christianity today. Other uncomfortable relationships have also been developed over the years between Christian ministers and Unity.

This kind of action fulfills the desire of the founders of Unity School of Christianity, Charles and Myrtle Fillmore. Mr. Fillmore said that his movement was "going into the orthodox church, and a great awakening will take place in Christianity."[1] It has long been a standing plan of Unity to have people stay in their respective denominations while promulgating Unity doctrines.[2] Unity has the appearance of Christianity. While it actually denies salvation by grace through the shed blood of Jesus, Unity, in alliance with metaphysical cults and the New Age Movement, diminishes the Bible, depersonalizes God, makes Jesus a common man, elevates mankind to godhood, and makes salvation the result of human efforts and reincarnation.

WHY DO PEOPLE JOIN CULTS?

I traveled to Unity Village on several occasions to collect information and learn about the people. When I arrived at Unity Village, one of the first things I noticed was the care taken in maintaining the grounds. The lawns are neatly manicured, the shrubs are trimmed, the flowers are in bloom, and sidewalks are free of litter. The buildings that dot the campus are always busy with people going to and fro.

What attracts so many people to Unity? Why have so many people left Christian churches to make Unity their home? One clue to answering these questions was given by a former student and resident of Unity Village who is now a Christian. "It was the love," she said, "which first enticed me into Unity. I was in a place of just having been divorced and I was feeling down about myself. Unity says that you are special and needed. They teach you how to love yourself and others."

This former student is correct. It is not unusual for people to innocently begin to read material from a cult, like Unity, and then join it because the message appears to answer their needs. I have identified four main reasons why people join Unity and other cults. These reasons fall into the following categories: *spiritual, personal, intellectual, and social.* Disregarding those who join cults because they were born into them, we find that these categories provide the reasons for most other joiners.

Spiritual reasons tend to be at the top of the list. Mankind was created as both a spiritual and physical being (Gn 1:26-27; 2:7). Our spiritual nature was made in the image and likeness of God. Mankind fell into sin through Adam and Eve, so sin was passed on to all (Gn 3:1-19; Rom 5:12-14).

We naturally have a spiritual void through Adam's disobedience. Mankind's history is filled with attempts at filling this void. The cults have tried to provide answers to spiritual needs and to draw those who are seeking such an answer.

Many who join cults are spiritually dissatisfied with their present church, so they begin to look at the alternatives the cults provide. The Christian church has the true answer to man's spiritual problems, but often we have failed to meet those needs through proper teaching of the Word of God (Mt 28:19).

Personal reasons for joining a cult fall close behind the spiritual. The nature of man is such that we have emotional needs. The former Unity student we spoke of gave this for her reason. She was hurt from a divorce. She needed love and compassion. Unity came to her rescue and tried to fill that need.

One other personal reason why people join cults is that they are grieving over the death of a loved one. Their minds are full of questions about the hereafter and they lose hope. The cults provide simplistic answers about life, death, and immortality. During this period of emotional stress, these people become subject to false teachings and the false hope connected with them.

The Bible tells us that the greatest command for the Christian is to love (Mk 12:30-31). When we fail to do this, the person in need becomes prey for the cults. Faith, hope, and love can only be properly rooted in the gospel of Jesus Christ (1 Cor 13).

There are so-called intellectual reasons why some people join cults. There can be little doubt that the liberal theologian Marcus Bach led many people into Unity through his book. Many trusted him as a Protestant writer. He made the claim several times that Unity answered his intellectual wrestlings. In his chapter on the Unity view of reincarnation, he frankly said, "In my research among the many religions of the world, few brought the spirit of living so fully in the whole spectrum of life as Unity does."[3]

Most intellectual questions that people ask about Christianity are fully answered in the Bible. The rebellious nature of man keeps him from accepting these answers. Some people reject the gospel message because of ignorance and blindness of their hearts (Eph 4:17). Others are always asking questions and are never able to come to a knowledge of the truth (2 Tm 3:7). God is certainly not against us asking questions and looking for answers. He gave us brains, intelligence, reasoning powers, and even demonstrated logical precepts (like the law of noncontradiction). The cults lead people outside of his Word into vain philosophies, after the tradition of men (Col 2:8).

There are social reasons why people join cults. The first is that it is our nature to need each other, to be part of a social unity. Proverbs 18:24 says, "A man of many companions may come to ruin but there is a friend who sticks closer than a brother." Most of us like the idea of togetherness, and the Bible makes provision for the social needs that we have. Fellowship in the church as the community of believers provides this (Heb 10:25). Sometimes Christians sin by shunning those who are poor and in need of fellowship (Jas 2:1-9).

Many cults were founded by former Protestants who were dissatisfied with their churches. This is the story of the Unity School of Christianity. Charles Fillmore was raised as an Episcopalian and Myrtle Fillmore was raised a strict Methodist. The Fillmores turned away from the sound teaching of the Bible and began their own movement, one with New Age metaphysics at its core.

THE HISTORY OF UNITY

Charles Fillmore, born August 22, 1854, was raised in the pioneer era of Minnesota. He had little formal education but became an avid reader. Even though he was raised Episcopalian, much of what he read was on spiritualism and the occult. He may have been influenced by a friend who was a self-proclaimed medium. They would spend many evenings together with their fingers pressed lightly on a table top in the attempt to raise the table or "table tapping" as it is known in occult circles.[4]

Mr. Fillmore went into business as a real estate broker before he met his first wife, Myrtle. He built quite a financial base, and this provided the necessary income to support them in the early days of Unity.

Mary Caroline "Myrtle" Page was born August 6, 1845. She was raised a Methodist and was very active in her church through the first few years of their marriage. She was well educated and went to Oberlin College to prepare for a teaching career.

Charles and Myrtle were married in 1881. They were both stricken with serious illnesses early in their marriage. Myrtle, who had tuberculosis, sought healing through attending a lecture in Kansas City, Missouri, given by Dr. Eugene B. Weeks in the spring of 1886. Dr. Weeks was a metaphysics teacher from the Illinois Metaphysical College, headed by Emma Curtis Hopkins, in Chicago.

Myrtle came out of the meetings claiming the affirmation, "I am a child of God and therefore I do not inherit sickness."⁵ Within one year of that date, she was completely cured of her tuberculosis.

Charles, being somewhat skeptical, wanted to investigate metaphysics for himself. He went to Chicago to study under Hopkins at her college. He came back as a teacher and later admitted that, together, the Fillmores had taken more than forty courses in metaphysics.⁶

In 1889 they launched their first publication called *Modern Thought*. It carried a variety of articles on religion, such as Buddhism, Hinduism, Theosophy, Rosicrucianism, Christianity, and the occult. In later issues of the magazine Fillmore renounced spiritualism, magnetism, hypnotism, mesmerism, and astrology.⁷

His magazine had a rough beginning and changed names several times. He called the second edition *Christian Science Thought*. Mary Baker Eddy, the founder of Christian Science, sued the Fillmores over the name in 1890. She won the rights to the name, so he renamed his publication *Thought*. This lasted one year when he added the word Unity to the name and it became *Unity and Thought*. It was not until 1898 that *Unity* became the permanent title, which it carries today.

The Fillmores started the School of Practical Christianity in 1903 and changed that name to Unity School of Christianity in 1914.

In the beginning Unity was part of the larger New Thought movement. New Thought was the common designation for metaphysical groups. Ralph Waldo Emerson used the words "this new thought" in reference to his transcendentalism. The metaphysical teacher M. John Murray popularized the term about 1900 with the phrase, "The New Thought of Man, the Larger Thought of God." Most New Thought teachings can be traced back to Phineas Parker Quimby (1802-1868) who conducted early experiments in healing through the mind.[8] Today these movements have become a worldwide confederation known as the New Age movement.

Fillmore was tied into the International New Thought Federation until 1906, when he broke away over divergent goals. Unity rejoined the alliance in 1919, only to break away again in 1922. They have remained separate organizations since then.

Unity publishes three magazines, *Unity, Daily Word*, and *Wee Wisdom*. The *Daily Word* [9] is by far the most successful of the three. It is printed in ten languages and disseminated in one hundred fifty-three countries. *Wee Wisdom* is a children's magazine which sprang out of Myrtle Fillmore's teaching career.

Unity was a pioneer in religious radio broadcasting in the 1920s. They purchased one of the most powerful midwest radio stations in Kansas City in 1924. *The Word*, their radio program, is heard on six hundred thirteen stations in North America. Their most recent venture has been one-minute television spots which have been airing nationwide.

The headquarters for Unity has become a small town of its own. What began as the purchase of a farm sixteen miles south of Kansas City in 1920 has turned into a complex of buildings and dormitories. Named Unity Village, the site has its own post office to handle the heavy volume of mail, and a prayer tower where prayer is held by the faithful, twenty-four hours each day.

UNDERSTANDING METAPHYSICS

Metaphysical rhetoric is not always easy to comprehend. Metaphysical teachers speak and write in such esoteric language that one usually needs a metaphysical dictionary to understand them. Unity publishes its own *Metaphysical Bible Dictionary*, by Charles Fillmore.

A sampling from this dictionary under the heading of *Jehovah* will illustrate just how complex their jargon is. "Creation," he says, "originates and exists in Divine Mind, God. In the creative process Divine Mind first ideates [sic] itself. In the Scripture this ideal is named Jehovah, meaning I AM the ever living, He who is eternal. The creation is carried forward through the activity of the Holy Spirit."[10]

This was Fillmore's complete statement about creation and Jehovah. In simpler terms, he said that God forms a plan for creation. Jehovah brings the plan into manifestation and the Holy Spirit helps to perfect it.

One of the major problems I have successfully pointed out to a number of metaphysicians like Unity followers and New Agers is that they would not be able to pass a college course or a driver's license exam, for that matter, if they read it in the same way they read their Bible.

This is not the case with Christianity. It has long been a rule of biblical interpretation that we read the Bible in its ordinary normal sense because the Bible is literally truth set in historical context. To echo the Christian theologian Clark Pinnock, "What we have left when we leave the literal sense is generally non-sense."[11]

The difference between the metaphysical interpretation and the literal interpretation is that the metaphysician sees the Word of God *behind* the text, whereas the Christian sees the Word of God *in* the text and *as* the text.

The literalness of the Bible is evident in that no historical passage of the Old Testament was ever used allegorically or spiritualized by Jesus and the apostles. We learn our rules of interpretation from them.

Even when a figure of speech or a parable is used in the Bible it is done to convey a literal truth about the situation. We do the same thing today. We say, without qualification, that the sun rose at 6:15 A.M. and set at 8:05 P.M. In actuality it did not rise or set, it was stationary the whole time. Within this figure of speech, though, is the literal and ordinary sense that if you look eastward at 6:15 A.M. you will see the sun on the horizon.

Denials of the authenticity of the Bible are plentiful in Unity. Eric Butterworth, past president of the Unity Ministers' Association, said, "One of the greatest limitations to understanding the Bible is to insist on its infallibility."[12] His mentor, Charles Fillmore, said, "He [Jesus] never authorized a history of his own life as recorded in the

Gospels...." He went further by condemning Christians for reading "the Bible in the letter instead of the spirit...."[13]

If Unity teaches that the Bible is not infallible, they should be asked why they use the Bible at all. When I have asked Unity ministers for the criterion that determines which part of the Bible should be adhered to or shunned, I usually get no response. It is obvious that there is no criterion for such a statement in Unity. If there is no method in Unity to assure them that any particular text is sound, how would they know if their spiritual interpretation is based upon a text which is faulty? Their whole system of metaphysical interpretation begins to crumble if the text is not known to be valid. The interpretation of an invalid text would be invalid also.

We find two problems in Mr. Fillmore's statement that Jesus never authorized his own history. It first assumes that what was written about Jesus in the Gospels was intended as a history. The second assumption is that if we do not have a statement of authorization by Jesus, it somehow would make what has been written less valid and untrue. President Lincoln may not have authorized a history of himself, but that does not mean that what we read about President Lincoln is untrue.

I believe we can find open acknowledgments by Jesus that he expected his disciples to write the Gospels. He said, "But the Counselor, the Holy Spirit, whom the Father will send in my name, will teach you all things and will remind you of everything I have said to you" (Jn 14:26).

In the first three chapters of the book of Revelation, which was one of the last books written in the New Testament (A.D. 95), we find Jesus referring to "my Word" which the church had. In chapter 3 he speaks to the church of Philadelphia, located in what is southwest Turkey today. He commends them for keeping "my Word" and "my command." Where would they get his Word and command if it had not been written for them? All through these chapters Jesus continually told John, "Write these things down" (Rv 1:11, 19; 2:1, 8, 12, 18; 3:1, 7, 14).

The most interesting statement occurs when Jesus quotes Luke's writings in Revelation 2:24. The book of Acts, written by Luke, was quoted by Jesus to the church of Thyatira (located in western Turkey). Why should they know the book of Acts and be responsible for what it said? It is obvious that Jesus knew they had it and that it contained historical information about him (Acts 1, 2, 4). Luke referred to his own Gospel in the first verse of Acts. Had Jesus not approved of the Gospels, then this would not have been so. John also acknowledged that the things he wrote were "what we heard from him and declare to you" (1 Jn 1:5).

Mr. Fillmore challenged the Christian church for interpreting the Bible literally, accusing us of having the letter and not the spirit of the Word. This is not true. Fillmore's reference is found in 2 Corinthians 3:6, which says, "who made us competent as ministers of a new covenant, not of the letter, but of the Spirit, for the letter kills, but the Spirit gives life." The context of 2 Corinthians chapter 3 has nothing to do with literal or spiritual interpretation of the Bible. Mr. Fillmore has taken this verse out of its context where, properly understood, the letter is a reference to the old covenant and the Spirit is a reference to the new covenant.

To best understand metaphysical thinkers you must realize that they tend to look for a spiritual truth behind what is said. This is stated in the preface of Fillmore's *Metaphysical Bible Dictionary.* "By 'metaphysics,' " he said, "we refer to the inner or esoteric meaning of the name defined."[14]

When they refer to the science of the mind, they mean, "the systematic and orderly arrangement of knowledge."[15] They believe that Jesus was a metaphysician who "worked out step by step in His three years' ministry spiritual and mental formulas which we can apply and . . . finally attain the perfect expression of the divine-ideal man. . . ."[16]

THE THEOLOGY OF UNITY

Unity has never published a theological work on their beliefs because they consider systematic theology to be less important than personal experience. There was only one time that Charles Fillmore wrote a statement of faith for Unity. Even then he qualified it by saying that "we shall not be bound by this tentative statement of what Unity believes." He added, "We may change our mind tomorrow on some of the points, and if we do, we shall feel free to make a new statement."[17] A new statement was never written.

God is abstract and impersonal in Unity. Fillmore gave this as one of his definitions for God: "The truth is, then, that God is Principle,

Law, Being, Mind, Spirit, All-God, Omnipotent, Omniscient, Omnipresent, Unchangeable, Creator, Father, Cause and Source of all that is."[18]

The terms in this definition which are common in Christianity take on completely different meanings in Unity. Father, in Unity, is not the loving Person of the Bible.[19] Rather, they use Father to mean an impersonal Mind which only takes on personal significance when expressed through the human. Since he is not a person, he has no love of his own. His love only becomes personal when it is expressed through the individual. The Father becomes the source for the love which we show and only in this way does he take on a personality.

Many Christians have misunderstood the Unity concept of God. They usually equate Unity with pantheism, meaning that God is the material world. Unity is actually panentheism, where God is a part of the world in the way that the mind or soul is a part of the body. Panentheism has been well refuted by Dr. Norman Geisler in his book, *Christian Apologetics*.[20]

Unity does not say that God is the material universe, such as classical pantheism does. Unity says that God is the "real thing standing under every visible form of life."[21] H. Emilie Cady, an authoritative Unity writer, says that the visible things, such as rocks, trees, and animals, are manifestations of the one Spirit.[22] She explains this further in another book, "He lives within every created thing at very center as the life. . . . This is not pantheism, which declares that the visible universe . . . is God."[23]

The importance of this distinction cannot be overlooked. If you or I were to suggest to a Unity member that Unity is pantheistic, he or she will turn a deaf ear toward all that we say. The Unity member feels that if you are so "unenlightened" as to have mistaken his or her beliefs as pantheistic, then what new truth could you share with him or her?

Unity sees no distinction between the names of gods in world religions and the God of the Bible. Fillmore says, "God, or Primal Cause, is good. It does not make any great difference what you name this Primal Cause. . . . The Hindoo calls it Brahm . . . ."[24] Jesus Christ, he says, "is known under various names in the many religious systems. The Krishna of the Hindoo is the same as the Christos of the Greeks and the Messiah of the Hebrews."[25]

Since Unity denies that God is personal, they have to redefine the three persons of the Trinity. Fillmore said, "The religious know this as Father, Son, and Holy Spirit; to the metaphysician it is Mind, Idea, Expression." Stated in another way, "The Father is Principle. The Son is Principle revealed in a creative plan. The Holy Spirit is the executive power of both Father and Son carrying out the creative plan."[26]

In creation, the Mind (Father) conceives an Idea (Son). This Idea (Son) is like a pattern, or plan, to create visible objects. The Expression (Holy Ghost) is the wisdom to know how these visible objects are formed and manifested.

When we look at Jesus Christ in Unity, we first have to divide the terms and make Jesus one thing and Christ another. This is typical of most metaphysical and New Age cults. Jesus is seen as a man who discovered the way to get released from reincarnation. Christ is seen as the "real self of all men."[27] Jesus just happened to discover how to tap into the power of his inner "Christ" and resurrect his body. According to Unity it is our job to do the same thing Jesus did and discover the "Divine Mind . . . true, spiritual, higher self . . ." within us.[28]

Unity's view of Jesus is that he was in search of salvation for himself, just as any other human. Charles Fillmore claimed that the reincarnations of Jesus were "His days in school."[29] A former student of Unity's religious school said they were taught that "a person had to be reincarnated twenty times. Jesus reached perfection because he had died nineteen other times before."

The Holy Spirit in Unity is seen as the law of God in action. It was taught by Fillmore that the Holy Spirit takes on personality, such as speaking, leading, reproving, and comforting.[30] This should not be confused with the biblical concept that the Holy Spirit is a person. Unity still teaches that the Holy Spirit is not a person, but only functions with the characteristics of a person.

The best way I have found to share what the Bible says about God with a Unity member is to ask questions. These questions should center around why a certain passage about God is taken spiritually instead of literally. We have the evidence that the texts of the Bible can be trusted.[31] Unity lacks any evidence that it should be trusted.

Charles Fillmore prided himself on the logic of Unity. "The one important thing the student of spiritual science must learn is to trust the logic of the mind."[32] There are many underlying fallacies with his system. Primarily, God's love becomes a meaningless term in Unity. Cady said, "God is Love. . . . All the love in the universe is God."[33] God in Unity is impersonal and cannot truly love anyone. He is only the source of love which we humans share with each other.

Let me illustrate the fallacy with electricity. By itself electricity is static energy and impersonal. If I shock another person with static electricity, it did not suddenly become personal just because it was shared between two humans. Love is an emotional characteristic of personality. If God loves, as the Bible says, then he must be a person as well. God demonstrates his love (Rom 5:8), he loves us with great love (Eph 2:4), God loved the world (Jn 3:16), and the Father himself loves us (Jn 14:21, 23; 16:27). These are just a few examples of God acting in love as well as being the source of love. This approach may be carried out with many of the other attributes of God which Unity has spiritualized. Showing a Unity member that God is a personal Being is important.

The Christ in the Bible is not an eternal principle idealized in Jesus. Christ is the Greek form of the Hebrew word for Messiah. It had only one meaning throughout Scripture—the anointed one. There was only one Messiah predicted throughout the Old Testament. He came into the world as Jesus and was called Christ from his birth (Lk 2:11). Jesus said that many false prophets will come in the last days saying that they are Christ (Mt 24:3-5, 11, 24). This is fulfilled in the metaphysical groups which claim that we all have Christ in us. First John 2:22 strongly tells us that Jesus is not a Christ, but the only Christ: "Who is the liar but he who denies that Jesus is the Christ?"

SALVATION AND REINCARNATION

Unity teaches a form of reincarnation. Unlike Hinduism, they do not believe in transmigration, from animals to humans. They only believe in human souls going to new humans.

They also have a new twist on the resurrection of Jesus. Unity teaches that Jesus raised his own body both physically and spiritually. The resurrection is seen as the goal of Unity followers because it is the perfection of the body. According to Fillmore, Jesus is still somewhere on earth in spirit form, and when he wills to, he manifests a physical body like he did for his disciples. "Jesus," he says, "did not leave the planet, at his Ascension; he simply entered the inner spiritual realms."[34]

Forgiveness of sins comes in Unity by denial of sins. Fillmore says, joy comes when "the mind has been cleansed by denial of sin."[35] He does not see the atonement of Jesus as the covering for our sins. "The atonement," he writes, ". . . has not taken sin, suffering, and death from the world."[36] He also denies that the blood of Jesus cleanses us from sin, ". . . the red blood of the flesh does not carry the power to 'cleanse your conscience from dead works . . .' "[37] The only way which Unity provides for its people to be free from sin is to deny sin. *Unity* magazine in January, 1936, printed this affirmation for members to recite: "I am not a sinner. I never did sin. I am from above."

Parallel with the Unity concept of sinlessness is their teaching that we are gods, part of the Divine Mind. Jesus, they say, "revealed to men their godhood."[38] "Ye are gods," they tell their followers, by taking Jesus' statement out of context.[39] "Individualize yourself in the highest," Fillmore writes, "by affirming that in Spirit and in Truth you are all that God is."[40] Sadly, Unity has fallen into the same trap that caused Adam and Eve to fall in the Garden of Eden when they were tempted to become like God (Gn 3:5).

What does Unity look for in salvation? Fillmore says that it was to "resurrect our body just as Jesus resurrected his."[41] He writes, "We know that the law of life is based in mind-action, and that through the mind we may resurrect ourselves from the dead."[42] Salvation in the Bible is completely different from Unity teaching. The Bible teaches that all are sinners and have no hope of saving themselves. "For all have sinned and fall short of the glory of God" (Rom 3:23); "he saved us, not because of righteous things we have done, but because of his mercy. He saved us, through the washing of rebirth and renewal by the Holy Spirit" (Ti 3:5); ". . . and the blood of Jesus, his Son, purifies us from all sin" (1 Jn 1:7); "If we say that we have no sin, we deceive ourselves, and the truth is not in us" (1 Jn 1:8); "If we claim we have not sinned, we make him out to be a liar and his word has no place in our lives" (1 Jn 1:10).

The resurrection of Jesus Christ was not the last cycle of reincarnation, it was the refutation of reincarnation. Hebrews 9:27 says it is appointed unto man but once to die, and after this the judgment. First Corinthians 15 is known as the resurrection chapter because Paul deals with the subject in detail. All throughout this chapter Paul speaks of only two bodies, the natural and the spiritual. We do not have many natural bodies before the resurrection.

Unity attempts to line up their view of reincarnation with the Bible. The following biblical topics will show its incompatibility: They assume that the personal identity of the individual is a part of God. The Bible tells us that our spirits are not eternal, but were created by God: Gn 2:7; Job 33:4; Is 43:7; 45:12; Zec 12:1; Mt 10:28; 1 Cor 15:48-49.

They assume the preexistence of man's soul for it to reincarnate several times. The Bible does not allow for the preexistence of the soul: Jn 3:13; 8:23; 1 Cor 15:44-46; Eph 4:7-9.

They assume that death is not the final state before judgment. The Bible shows that we only live once: Is 14:9-11; Mk 9:43-48; Lk 16:27-29; Acts 7:59; 2 Cor 5:8; Phil 1:23.

CONCLUSION

The Fillmores have set up a system of belief by taking what they thought were the logical and best principles of all religions. "Logic is necessary," Charles Fillmore says, "you must trust logic." We have shown Unity beliefs to be both unscriptural and lacking logical continuity.

When we share the gospel with Unity members, we need to help them understand why they need to take the words of Jesus as the ultimate truth. God's communications to us through his Word have no hidden, esoteric meanings. The book of 1 John uses the words "we know" twenty-eight times in refutation to those who claim a higher knowledge than Scripture. What we know is what "we have heard ... seen ... and handled" (1 Jn 1:1-3).

Charles Fillmore was not even sure where his information came from. "I received unexpected revelations ... I do not remember that I asked who the author of my guidance was; I took for granted that it was Spirit."[43] He did not have the confidence of the writers of the New Testament, who knew Jesus personally.

"God and I can somehow communicate," he said, "or the whole thing is a fraud."[44] The way in which we know that Charles Fillmore did not hear from God is to compare what he claimed with what we know was from God, the Bible. We have done this here and we need to share it with those in Unity. Jesus can save them by his wonderful grace, just as he has done for many others.

NINE

Scientology

Kurt Van Gorden

M OST MAN-MADE RELIGIONS are founded by someone who claims to be a holy man. The Church of Scientology, however, makes no such claim. Their founder, L. Ron Hubbard, was a popular science fiction writer of the 1930s and 1940s who made a "sudden" career change in 1950 by publishing *Dianetics: A Modern Science of Mental Health*. Mr. Hubbard's writing career still flourished, but his subject matter changed from science fiction novels to self-help psychotherapy and religious matter for the Church of Scientology.

Lafayette Ronald Hubbard, born March 13, 1911 in Tilden, Nebraska, had predicted his own career change during a science fiction convention in 1949. While he was speaking to the group, he reportedly said, "Writing for a penny a word is ridiculous. If a man really wanted to make a million dollars, the best way would be to start his own religion."[1] The first edition of *Dianetics* was released the following year. It was in 1951 that Mr. Hubbard published his first book on Scientology and followed it with the incorporation of the Church of Scientology of California, February 18, 1954. These quick moves by Mr. Hubbard helped dianetics and Scientology become a worldwide religion of six million adherents. Many former Scientologists point out that the number of active adherents is much less, ranging anywhere from two hundred thousand to two million.[2]

During the last several years of his life, the science fiction writer turned religionist lived the life of a recluse, his whereabouts shrouded in mystery. On January 24, 1986, he died of a cerebral hemorrhage and his remains were cremated. The controversial Mr. Hubbard is gone, but the church he founded is probably here to stay. For this reason we need to examine Scientology from the perspective of biblical faith. If Hubbard expounded biblical truth, we should uphold it; if he taught error, then we should expose it.

DIANETICS: FORERUNNER OF SCIENTOLOGY

Hubbard was a prolific writer who regularly made up new terms and redefined others for special use in his writings. Nearly all Scientology publications contain a glossary full of definitions. Hubbard even wrote his own dictionary to help the Scientologist work his way through his material.

Dianetics was readily received by the public upon its release. Anticipations had mounted through a pre-publication synopsis of his theories in a pulp-magazine, *Astounding Science Fiction*, May, 1950. Readers of the magazine were already familiar with Hubbard as a spellbinding writer. His newest venture, *Dianetics*, did not have the usual flowing style of his novels. Rather, it was replete with scientific jargon and pop-psychology theories about the mind and mental health therapy. Its success was so overwhelming that *Publisher's Weekly* reported that fifty-five thousand copies were sold in the first two months and over seven hundred fifty dianetics groups had started nationwide.[3]

In *Dianetics*, Hubbard announced his new therapy as a "science of mind," which promised to "clear" a person of aberrations, painful experiences, and mental illness.[4] The clear person, he said, "can be tested for all psychoses, neuroses, compulsions, and repressions (all aberrations) and can be examined for any autogenetic (self-generated) diseases referred to as psychosomatic ills. These tests confirm the clear to be entirely without such ills or aberrations. Additional tests of his intelligence indicate it to be high above the current norm."[5]

Hubbard's theory is based upon several views of mankind and

his behavior. One of the first premises is that man is basically good.[6] The goal of any man is survival; evil, pain, psychosomatic illness, and aberrations (irrational behavior) all contribute to man's failure at survival.[7] The mind has three major divisions, according to Hubbard. The Analytical Mind is that which works like a perfect computer. It analyzes data and is similar to Freud's conscious mind. It is the person, the "I."[8] The Reactive Mind is the "portion of the mind which works on a totally stimulus-response basis."[9] It is the entire source of aberration and irrational behavior. We could liken it to the subconscious mind. The third is the Somatic Mind, which is directed by the Analytical and Reactive Minds. It places solutions into effect on the physical plane.[10]

Hubbard's theory states that the analytical mind is what controls and commands the human being. This is called the fully "conscious" person. The analytical mind seldom uses its full potential because of the interference from the reactive mind. Any time the awareness of the analytical mind is reduced through pain, emotional shock, or a similar event, the reactive mind takes over. He calls this a moment of "unconsciousness."[11] It is during these partially unconscious states that the pre-clear receives complete picture-like images of his immediate surroundings. This is called an "engram," which Hubbard originally said was recorded on the protoplasm of our cells. While the analytical mind is a computer-like memory, the reactive mind does not have a memory, but only picture-like engrams which are filed in successive order.

These engrams are counterproductive to our survival. They are the root cause, says Hubbard, of all our aberrations. They make us "mad, ineffective, and ill."[12] The auditor asks leading questions, called commands, and listens to the pre-clear's response. Once all the engrams are removed, he is pronounced clear.

Being clear of engrams will raise your IQ, cure the common cold, give you complete recall of everything you have ever studied, and speed up your computations one hundred twenty times faster than normal.[13] Hubbard lists a few additional benefits of being clear. It will correct poor eyesight, remove calcium deposits, stop ringing ears, and save marriages.[14]

Not everyone was willing to acknowledge such sweeping payoffs for this unconventional therapy. The media spoke out against it by interviewing Hubbard's opponents. With the younger population, however, it became faddish to audit friends at dianetic parties.

John W. Campbell, Jr., the editor of *Astounding Science Fiction*, had published several of Hubbard's science fiction stories. When Hubbard first told Campbell about his new science of the mind, Campbell became an instant convert. At that time Campbell was suffering from sinusitis (infection of the lining of the sinuses) and was treated by dianetic therapy. He became so enthusiastic about the possibilities for dianetics that he announced its coming in his April, 1950, issue.

Campbell had a friend who was a medical doctor in Michigan, Dr. Joseph Agasta Winter. He introduced Dr. Winter to dianetics and eventually to Hubbard. Dr. Winter applied dianetic therapy to his six-year-old son who had a fear of darkness and ghosts. His son's phobias were gone, so Dr. Winter sold his practice and moved to New Jersey to help Hubbard promote dianetics. He wrote the introduction to the first edition of *Dianetics*.[15]

Neither man's allegiance to Hubbard lasted long. The August, 1951, issue of *Astounding Science Fiction* carried the last of a series of dianetics promotions. Isaac Asimov, who knew both Campbell and Hubbard, related a conversation he had with Campbell about parting company with Hubbard. "He had broken with Hubbard and was out of the Dianetics movement."[16] Campbell's sinusitis was never cured.

Dr. Winter broke away from Hubbard's movement in October, 1950, and wrote a book with his own concepts of how to heal mental illness. Dr. Winter, who claimed that Hubbard was "absolutistic and authoritarian,"[17] gave several reasons for leaving the movement. His most important reason was that no one had become clear through dianetics. He may have been referring to the grandiose event held at Shriner's Auditorium in Los Angeles, August 10, 1950, when Hubbard announced Sonia Bianca as the world's first clear. The event failed miserably. Miss Bianca, a physics major from Boston, was paraded before a full auditorium of press representatives and curiosity seekers. When questions were put to her, she could not remember a basic physics formula or the color of Hubbard's necktie, which she had seen moments before. The total recall of the clear floundered so badly that Hubbard did not announce another cleared person until 1966.[18]

SCIENTOLOGY: THE TRANSITION TO A CHURCH

Things began to tumble like dominoes for Hubbard. His first clear failed. Campbell left him. Winter left him. Hubbard's second wife divorced him. And Dr. Roodenberg, head of the New York office for dianetics, left after charging Hubbard with refusing "to document his cases with medical supporting evidence."[19] If we add to this the criticisms of the medical profession and media, it becomes apparent that Hubbard was facing a problem his first year after *Dianetics* was published.

His resourcefulness at "discovering" new technology in a time of need paid off. He added the word "Scientology" to his growing list of newly constructed terms. Dianetics, he said, means "through the soul." Scientology, he added, means "the study of knowledge in its fullest sense."

One of Hubbard's new concepts introduced through Scientology is that man is a spirit being called a Thetan. He calls the physical universe MEST, for Matter, Energy, Space, and Time. Additional courses are offered for survival through Hubbard's eight dynamics of life: self, sex, group, mankind, other life forms, MEST, spirits, and a Supreme Being. After one becomes clear he must strive to become an Operating Thetan (OT), which means that he has control over MEST. A process similar to astral projection was introduced, called exteriorization. Searching for reincarnated engrams through your Thetan's past lives became routine.[20]

About the same time a new dimension of auditing was introduced. Volney Mathison, who had already been a follower of dianetics, invented an electronic instrument, for which Hubbard coined a thirty-two letter word, the "electroencephaloneurometimograph." Hubbard quickly saw the value of Mathison's invention for engram tracking, and he wrote a book on how to use it in auditing the pre-clear.

It went through two name changes before it was dubbed the E-Meter. Hubbard had already been experimenting with lie-detecting devices, but none were shown to be as reliable as the E-Meter.[21] It was a transistorized galvanometer consisting of ordinary tin cans connected by wires. The pre-clear holds the tin cans while the auditor sits on the opposite side of the counseling table watching the E-Meter needle.

As they talk back and forth, the auditor gives new commands to the pre-clear. Various needle reactions cue the auditor to go to an earlier chain of engrams. The goal of the session is to erase the engrams. This is indicated when the needle "floats," moving back and forth slowly after the same command has been given. The E-Meter gives a more scientific appearance to Scientology though it remains a questionable instrument.[22]

SCIENTOLOGY BECOMES A RELIGION

The rapid development of dianetics and Scientology in the early 1950s caught some people by surprise. *Time* magazine, however, saw the writing on the wall when it suggested that "the cult of dianetics . . . has some of the features of a new religion."[23] Exactly twenty-nine months later the Church of Scientology of California was incorporated. There is no doubt that their dabbling in the supernatural and occultic spheres with recall of past lives, interplanetary travel, exteriorization, and other phenomena, gave religious overtones to Scientology.

In July, 1954, Hubbard held a series of lectures in Phoenix, Arizona, for his infant church. These were later published as *The Phoenix Lectures* and revealed the Hindu, Buddhist, and Taoist roots of Scientology.

From the Hindu Vedic hymns, Hubbard relates, "a great deal of our material in Scientology is discovered . . ."[24] He states, " Tao means Knowingness . . . it's an ancestor to Scientology, the study of 'knowing how to know.' "[25] Hubbard drew such a close relationship to Buddhism that he says the status of Bodhi, "intellectual and ethical perfection," would probably be "a Dianetic release."[26] Furthermore, Hubbard said that the Buddhist writings *Dhyana* "could be literally translated as 'Indian for Scientology,' if you wish to do that."[27]

Mr. Hubbard had difficulty convincing the world that dianetics was a genuine science. He had greater difficulty trying to convince the world that Scientology was a genuine religion. The Church of Scientology has entered into more court battles around the world than any other new religion. The U.S. Supreme Court had to declare Scientology as a *bona fide* religion to save it from IRS taxation. The question which concerns us here is not whether the Church of Scientology is a religion, but whether it is a false religion, by biblical standards.

THE THEOLOGY OF SCIENTOLOGY

Every group has its standard for authoritative writings. We understand that the Bible is the only rule for faith and conduct for Evangelical Christians. In Scientology the writings of L. Ron Hubbard are held in higher esteem than the Bible. His writings are said to be the fulfillment of ancient Buddhist prophecy. Hubbard himself said, the "truth of the matter is that you are studying an extension of the work of Gauthama Siddhartha, begun about 2,500 hundred years ago, . . . Buddha predicted that in 2,500 years the entire job would be finished in the West. . . . Well, we finished it!"[28]

Scientology claims that it "does not conflict with other religions or religious practices as it clarifies them and brings understanding of the spiritual nature of man."[29] When evangelizing Scientologists, you may be shown a few letters from people of various denominations who say that Scientology does not conflict with their beliefs in Christianity. The problem is that many of the people writing these kinds of letters do not believe in the Bible. No one who is faithful to God's Word can say that there are no conflicts between Scientology and the Bible. I have found that basic verses about Jesus' deity, Messianic fulfillment, death, and resurrection have no authority in the Scientologists' worldview.

One of the creeds of the Church of Scientology is "that all men have inalienable rights to their own religious practices and their performance."[30] When we evangelize Scientologists, we should never tell them they do not have the right to believe in and practice their religion. You can easily tell a Scientologist that you respect his right to believe as he wills, but respecting him does not mean that Scientology is true. The Bible tells us that open rebuke is better than love concealed (see Prv 27:5). If I really love my neighbor, as Jesus taught me, I will tell him what Jesus said: "if you do not believe that I am he, you will die in your sins" (Jn 8:24).

Establishing a source of authority while evangelizing Scientologists is important. In *The Phoenix Lectures,* Hubbard states that the Bible is based on the Egyptian *Book of the Dead* and is therefore a corrupted version of earlier pagan writings. However, while Hubbard questions the authority of the Bible, he simultaneously acknowledges certain passages to be true because he quotes them. When Scientologists study anything, they are taught not to go past any word they do not understand. This would be a good principle to use when you study the Bible with them. The best way for them to see the conflicts of authority between Hubbard and the Bible is to help them define biblical words correctly in their context. If you take each biblical concept, one at a time, and ask the Scientologist to study it with you, he will have no excuse for denying its truth. Some will still deny the Bible, but they will have no logical reason for doing so.

THE GODS OF SCIENTOLOGY

Some Scientology literature says that Scientology does not address the nature of God. Hubbard, in *Scientology: A World Religion Emerges in the Space Age* (Los Angeles: Church of Scientology, 1974 p. 17) states that "although the existence of the Supreme Being is affirmed in Scientology, His precise nature is not delineated, since the Church holds that each person must seek and know the Divine Nature in and for himself."

The Christian who witnesses to the Scientologist should not be distracted by this because the object is to point out the distinctions between what Scientology teaches and what Scripture says. The most obvious example is Hubbard's declaration of the existence of many gods. He wrote, "There are gods above all other gods...there is no argument here against the existence of a Supreme Being or any devaluation intended. It is that amongst the gods, there are many false gods elected to power and position. . . . There are gods above other gods, and gods beyond the gods of the universes."[31] Again, he says, "Let us take up what amounts to probably ten thousand years of study on the part of Man on the identity of God or gods, . . ."[32] Scientology does not tell its followers whether to believe in these other gods or not.

The Bible is emphatically opposed to the possibility of any gods other than the one true God. There is but one God—Deuteronomy

4:39; 6:4. There can be no god before him and none after him (Is 43:10). He does not know of any other god existing (Is 44:8). Many other passages reiterate the same: Mk 12:32; Eph 4:6; 1 Tm 2:5; Jas 2:19.

Hubbard once said, "for a long while some people have been cross with me for my lack of cooperation in believing in a Christian Heaven, God, and Christ."[33] But he claims that Christianity's concept of God is traced from Hindu writings. He says, "The Christian god is actually much better characterized in the Vedic Hymns than in any subsequent publication, including the Old Testament."[34]

God is described consistently the same in both the Old and New Testaments. There are two hundred forty-six Old Testament quotes in the New Testament to show this consistency. It is interesting that the Jews in the New Testament period never accused the Christians of not believing in their God, as Hubbard would have us believe.

Another area in conflict with biblical truth is the idea that men and women are a part of God. Hubbard describes man's composition this way, "A pre-clear is a precise thing, part animal, part pictures, and part God."[35] The ultimate end for man in Scientology is to become a "homo-novis," which Hubbard describes as "very high and godlike."[36]

Throughout the Bible there is an unclouded distinction between God and man. "God is not a man, that he should lie," Numbers 23:19 tells us. And "I am God, and not man, the Holy One in your midst" says Hosea 11:9.

When Hubbard said that man is "part God," he lacked an understanding of who God is in the Bible. God is eternal and not limited to eighty trillion, or any other number of years, like Hubbard's Thetan or spirit. Scripture points this out: "The eternal God is your refuge, and underneath are the everlasting arms," and once more, "God is great . . . Nor can the number of his years be discovered" (Dt 33:27; Job 36:26).

God is omnipotent and not limited in power like a Thetan. Jeremiah 32:17, speaking of God, says, "There is nothing too hard for you." The book of Job (42:2) adds, "I know that you can do everything, no plan of yours can be thwarted."

God is omniscient and not limited in knowledge like a Thetan. "For the Lord is the God of knowledge" 1 Samuel 2:3 tells us. Paul also writes, "Oh, the depth of the riches of the wisdom and knowledge of God! How unsearchable his judgments and his paths beyond tracing out!" (Rom 11:33).

God is omnipresent and not limited to the location of a Thetan. His omnipresence is expressed in Jeremiah 23:24, "Do I not fill heaven and earth?" Then, in 1 Kings 8:27, "The heaven, even the highest heaven, cannot contain you."

Scientology says that it allows each person to discover for himself what the Supreme Being is. The individual Scientologist may not believe all of Hubbard's statements about God or gods, but the false teachings are nonetheless present in his church. Treat the Scientologist as an individual and ask him what he believes about God or gods. Show him these Bible passages alongside Hubbard's statements and ask about the contradictions. God's grace for conversion can be present if you approach the Scientologist with prayer, patience, and preparation.

HUBBARD'S VIEW OF MAN

Hubbard borrowed his view of man from the Oriental philosophical concept, "I am not this body." He claimed that you are only a Thetan, or spirit being. In Scientology you only inhabit a body from time to time through your reincarnations. In the Christian church we recognize from the Old and New Testaments the dichotomy of man's nature. Biblically man is both a physical and spiritual being (Eccl 12:7); the two components are necessary to have a human being (Gn 2:7). To say that "I am not this body," is a contradiction, for without the body one could not make the statement. Subsequently, one must be more than just a spirit making the statement. If the spirit (or Thetan) cannot show its existence without a body, then the body is a necessary entity to prove existence. The body is a necessary part of the human.

The book of James says that the body without the spirit is dead (2:26). In Christianity we believe that disembodied human spirits go either to heaven or hades to await the resurrection of the just and unjust (Jn 5:29), whereupon they will be judged (Mt 25:31-32). The person is not complete again until the resurrection when the body is reunited with the spirit. Man was made as a body and spirit and is incomplete when these are separated through death.

Man's nature, according to Hubbard, is basically good. Hubbard abhorred the idea that man is sinful in his nature. In one *Auditor's Bulletin*, he said, "It is despicable and utterly beneath contempt to tell a man he must repent, that he is evil."[37] Elsewhere it is stated that, "Sin is composed of lies and hidden actions, and is therefore untruth."[38] Sins are recognized in Scientology but not as a result of man's evil nature. They say we have irrational behavior because of the "reactive mind."

In contrast to this the Bible shows us that we are sinful and evil in our basic nature. David, the Psalmist, knew that he had a sinful nature from the time of his conception (Ps 51:5). The book of Romans tells us, "There is no one who understands, . . . for all have sinned and fall short of the glory of God" (3:10, 23).

A DIFFERENT JESUS IN SCIENTOLOGY

Jesus Christ does not hold special significance in Scientology. In the Bible he is seen as an eternal, active person (Mi 5:2) who is one with the Father (Jn 10:30), second person of the Trinity (Mt 28:19). "In the beginning was the Word," John 1:1 opens, "and the Word was with God, and the Word was God." Most people can read John's first chapter and see that the Word is revealed as Jesus Christ, "The Word became flesh and dwelt among us . . . the only begotten of the Father" (Jn 1:14).

L. Ron Hubbard did not agree with the straightforwardness of John's Gospel. He only quoted part of the first verse, disregarding the context, and said that the Word was "Survival!"[39] In refutation to this we need only look at John 1:2 where the Word is given the personal pronoun "he." Hubbard's preliminary statement in each of his books "never go past a word you do not fully understand," fails when he misunderstood John 1:1.

Hubbard challenges the orthodox teaching about the life of Jesus by saying, "There is much speculation on the part of religious historians as to the early education of Jesus of Nazareth. It is believed by many authorities that Jesus was a member of the cult of the Essenes, who believed in reincarnation. . . ."[40] Again, he said, "Christ . . . was a bringer [sic] of information. He never announced his sources. He spoke of them as coming from God. But they might just as well have come from the god talked about in the Hymn to the Dawn Child . . . the Veda."⁴¹

When we look to the Bible we find that the things Jesus did were not done secretly (Acts 26:26). His life was not a legend or myth, it was historical. Peter specifically said that we do not follow cunningly devised fables, but we have irrefutable eyewitnesses (2 Pt 1:16).

SALVATION AND REINCARNATION

Salvation, according to Hubbard, is to be free from the endless cycle of birth and rebirth, reincarnation. This is done by erasing engrams through auditing. This could become a long and expensive process for the pre-clear, sometimes costing tens of thousands of dollars. The auditing becomes a very "real" experience for the Scientologist. This does not say that every real experience is valid. It would be easy for a Scientologist to test the validity of most auditing experiences just by talking with someone who was at the original event which he is supposed to have recalled.

The proof to many Scientologists that engrams are released during auditing is indicated by the accompanying signs. "When one releases an engram," Hubbard wrote, "the erasure is accompanied by yawns, tears, sweat, odor, panting, urine, vomiting, and excreta."⁴²

Scientology's view of reincarnation is different from many others, for it includes extraterrestrial life, evolution on other planets, evolution on earth, implant stations, forgetter implants, and engrams which keep us trapped in the reincarnation. Mr. Hubbard and Scientology have never allowed an unbiased blind or double blind control test to be conducted during their auditing sessions. If they did, it would show the same results that other testings on reincarnation have. There is no verification.⁴³

We find ample verification for events described in the Bible. The resurrection of Jesus Christ was eyewitnessed by unbelieving disciples on twelve different occasions (1 Cor 15:7). The guards of the tomb told the Jews about it (Mt 28:11). Jesus appeared to over five hundred people at one time (1 Cor 15:6). He appeared to an enemy of

Christianity, Saul (Acts 9:3-6). Peter preached the resurrection openly to the Jews who could not refute it (Acts 2:14, 31-36). Paul preached it to Festus the governor and to King Agrippa without refutation (Acts 25:19; 26:23-26).[44] The resurrection is a refutation of reincarnation because the resurrection shows that we will receive the body we have now, but in an immortal state. Reincarnation is forever laid to rest with Hebrews 9:27; "It is appointed for men to die once, but after this the judgment."

What every Scientologist is seeking is true salvation. It can only be found through believing in Jesus Christ as one's only Lord and Savior. Scientologists need to see themselves for who and what they really are. No one but Jesus lived a perfect sinless life (Heb 4:15). Jesus was sinless because he was God, second Person of the Trinity, in human flesh (Phil 2:6-8). He was pronounced holy from his birth (Lk 1:35). Though sinless, he willfully took our sins upon himself at the crucifixion (2 Cor 5:21). He purged our sins, resurrected his own body, and ascended to heaven, where he currently reigns (Heb 1:3; Rv 1:18).

We are inherently prone to sin because we have a sinful nature (Rom 5:12). Even though we try to do good, we eventually will do bad (Rom 7:13-25). Being unholy, there is no way we can stand in the presence of God, who is holy. We must have a covering for our sins to free us from the judgment and damnation which we deserve. God will forgive us of our sins if we cast ourselves upon his mercy and grace, trusting in the shed blood of Jesus instead of our own works (Tit 3:5; Eph 2:8-10; Rom 5:1-2).

When we approach the Scientologist with the gospel we must keep a few things in mind. Treat the Scientologist as an individual for whom Christ died. You may wish to share your testimony of how Jesus freed you from the bondage of sin and death, and how you know that you will live eternally with him (1 Jn 5:13).

Ask the Scientologist how long he has been involved in Scientology. If it has been six months or more you can be certain that he has had several experiences on the E-Meter, perhaps even into "past lives." These experiences are very real to him and should not be ridiculed. What you should do is begin to ask him to test the validity of the experiences. Ask him if he has ever had anything come up during auditing which left him questioning if it could have really happened. More than likely this has happened, but he may be reluctant to tell you.

Do not be afraid to give evidences for the reliability of the Bible. It will not take long for the Scientologist to realize that Hubbard's writings lack similar evidence. Use a modern translation of the Bible when you witness, and be willing to give him a copy if he does not have one. Frequently ask if he understood what was read because you may have to look up words for definition. Whenever a generalization or blanket statement is made by him, ask him to back it up. For example, many Scientologists have been taught that the early Christian church taught reincarnation and that later it was removed from the Bible. I simply ask them to provide the evidence for their claim. I have seen several Scientologists come to the conclusion that someone in Scientology deceived them. After nearly twenty years of witnessing to people in the cults, I have found that nothing is quite so powerful as a cultist making the self-discovery that his religious leader has misled him. The goal of the Christian is not merely to get cultists to realize they are wrong, but through prayer and guidance of the Holy Spirit to help them to find the truth of who Jesus our Savior is.

TEN

Confronting Cults
Cross-Culturally

Ruth Tucker

S EVERAL YEARS AGO a young couple responded to the call of God for missionary service with the Church of the Nazarene to serve in Martinique, a French island in the West Indies. There they became involved in a church-planting ministry that required countless hours of personal evangelism and community outreach. Out of their labors came a tiny church that gradually grew to the point of self-sufficiency. But while the missionaries were on a leave of absence, the little church was invaded by Jehovah's Witnesses. When they returned, they found that many of the people—including some of the leaders—had been swayed by the teachings of that cult and had joined with them. Their work was in shambles.

This story is repeated again and again. The characters and the settings change but the pattern is the same: unwary Christians are caught in a snare of deception masquerading as the herald of a more perfect or true or contemporary gospel. In Latin America, pastors are invited to posh vacation resorts for seminars on Unification Theology and are pulled into the web of Moon's worldwide Unification church. In Kenya, enthusiastic Mormons talk to Christian believers about Joseph Smith, "the Prophet of the hour," and about the *Book of Mormon*, "the most correct of any book on earth"— the "keystone" of their religion. In evangelistic crusades conducted by Luis Palau in Latin America, Asia, and Europe, cult members pose as crusade counselors and go house to house claiming that they are associated with his ministry. From Austria, Susanne Loucky opens her missionary prayer letter with the words: "First Impressions—Prevalence of Jehovah's Witnesses and Mormons."

The Cults Are Coming is the title of a recent book on cultic activity in America. It is a title that reflects the anxiety that many people feel toward cults. Such anxiety is warranted, considering the vigorous proselytizing done by Mormons, Jehovah's Witnesses, and others in our very neighborhoods, but an even more troublesome development is the reverse of that warning—*the cults are going*. In recent decades there has been an enormous increase of cultic missionary activity overseas—so much so that missionaries today are often as likely to confront someone from an American-based cult as they are someone from another world religion.

For most of the past century, America has had the distinction of being the world's leading sender of missionaries, and as a result, Christianity has penetrated every corner of the globe. But those very converts—be they in remote villages or teeming cities—are now threatened by a missionary zeal of the cults that in many instances surpasses that of Christian denominations. And as non-Western Christian churches increase their missionary outreach, so do cults that have been planted overseas. A vivid example of this is the present-day missionary work in Rarotonga. This tiny island in the South Seas was initially evangelized by John Williams, the great "Apostle of the South Seas." Later, another celebrated pioneer missionary, James Chalmers, ministered there for a decade. Christianity took hold, and soon natives of that island were reaching out as missionaries to neighboring islands.

Today that trend continues—native South Sea islanders reaching out to people on other islands—but with a different slant. An article in the *Saints Herald* tells one such story of a young couple and their three children. "Brother Buchin, a native of Tahiti, and Sister Teina, a native of the Cook islands" are "committed to . . . the island of Rarotonga"—"to share the gospel and to live among the people."[1] The gospel they share, however, is not the biblical faith of Christian orthodoxy. Rather, it is the "restored" gospel of Joseph Smith. The

Buchins are members of the Reorganized Church of Jesus Christ of Latter-day Saints (RLDS)—not the giant Mormon establishment of Salt Lake City, but the movement that followed Joseph Smith's widow, now headquartered in Independence, Missouri.

The evangelistic outreach in the South Seas is only a tiny portion of the vast RLDS mission enterprise worldwide—an enterprise that is energized by the church's underlying philosophy. Indeed, according to RLDS literature, "sharing the good news of God's redemption and care for all persons" is "the central purpose of the church."

But it is the LDS—the Utah Mormons—who are the most aggressive in their effort to spread the message of Joseph Smith. Today, after more than one hundred and fifty years of mission outreach, Mormonism is firmly planted throughout the world, fortified with temples and translated copies of the *Book of Mormon*.

MORMONISM

From a tiny band of zealots in 1830, Mormonism has spread out worldwide to become the largest pseudo-Christian cult in the world. From the earliest years the missionary impulse was strong. Mormons left their homes and carried out missionary work among Indians on the frontier and across the seas to the mother countries in Europe. They went in teams and entered communities in an attempt to saturate the area, family by family, with the "restored gospel." The usual and most fruitful method of evangelism was to win professing Christians to their point of view. An example of this occurred in Denmark, one of the Mormons' most productive mission fields. In 1850, Erastus Snow and three others opened up the work there by becoming part of a local Baptist church. One of the elderly Mormon converts, who later left the movement, wrote of how the converts were won:

> One Sunday we saw . . . four strangers enter the meeting hall and sit down near the doorway. No one paid any further attention to them or had any slightest inkling as yet regarding their intentions. But the sober, almost deferential piety which they showed, in common with all Americans, at religious

services, gave rise to a favorable opinion of them. They came frequently, made the acquaintance of the pastor and many members of the congregation, and gained admission to their homes, and then began little by little to speak about their mission, and they preached their new gospel. Their narrations concerning the miraculous call of the new prophet and his revelations naturally awakened great interest and discussion, and so Pastor Monster proceeded to an investigation of the matter. But Apostle Snow handled him so cleverly that he himself, without actually becoming a Mormon, seemed for a time to be altogether drawn in that direction and convinced the divine calling of the new prophet. . . .

The teachings of the missionaries found a fruitful soil among the Baptists. There was even talk of entire congregations going over to Mormonism, with Pastor Monster at their head. It did not actually go that far, but many did convert to the doctrine of the new apostle, and a new denomination was speedily organized under the name of "The Church of Jesus Christ of Latter-day Saints."[2]

The work in Denmark grew rapidly. In 1851, the *Book of Mormon* was translated into Danish. By 1853 the outreach had expanded to the point that the converts were divided into six branches. The work has continued unabated, and by the mid-1960s there were nearly two hundred missionaries assigned to the country.[3]

The recent surge in missionary outreach began in 1973 under the late President Spencer W. Kimball's administration. During a twelve-year period the number of countries with mission bases increased from fifty to ninety-six, and the missionary force, by 1981, had reached thirty thousand. The vast majority of the missionaries are young men who have volunteered for an eighteen-month assignment, to fulfill an obligation to their church. In the words of Kimball: "Every boy and many girls and couples should serve missions. Every prospective missionary should prepare morally, spiritually, mentally, and financially all of his life in order to serve faithfully, efficiently, and well in the Great Program of Missionary work. . . . A mission is not only a privilege and an opportunity but a solemn duty and obligation."[4]

Despite the short-term nature of the missionary endeavors, the work is concentrated and the number of converts reported is impressive. According to Mormon missiologist R. Lanier Britsch, "Most Mormon missionaries proselyte full-time, *i.e.,* 60 to 70 hours a week. Proselyting missionaries use several methods or combinations of methods in establishing contacts or teaching situations. House-to-house tracking, that is, knocking on doors and leaving printed information, is the most common approach."[5]

To accommodate the influx of converts worldwide, there has been a corresponding increase in the translations of the *Book of Mormon* and the building of temples. In 1985, a Mormon publication reported the completion of the seventieth translation. By 1989, that figure had grown to one hundred and sixty. By 1989, there were nearly fifty temples worldwide, nearly half of which had been built in the decade of the 1980s. In East Germany, a temple was being built at the very time the Berlin Wall was being torn down.[6]

Behind the facade of flawless success, however, are some serious problems. There are more drop-outs in the missionary force than the church would like to admit—partly due to the intense pressure for each missionary to win at least six converts a year. This pressure leads to shortcuts that reduce long-lasting results. In investigating Mormon missionary methods, Kenneth Woodward found that "the number and duration of conversions are highly ephemeral." He interviewed a former zone leader in Bolivia who admitted that dozens of Indian families were baptized by a Mormon missionary and later rebaptized by the next missionary on the circuit. Another problem he found was that of "Dolly baptisms—teenage girls who are more attracted by the missionaries than by the Holy Spirit and hope to come to the United States as wives."[7]

JEHOVAH'S WITNESSES

Though founded in the late nineteenth century, it was not until 1943, under the leadership of Nathan Homer Knorr, that the Jehovah's Witnesses developed a systematic global plan of missionary outreach. It was then that the Gilead Missionary Training School was founded to train full-time missionaries—more than seven thousand of whom have graduated to date. The statistics for present day worldwide outreach of the Jehovah's Witnesses is readily accessible through the annual *Yearbooks*, which indicate the growth—and lack of growth—of mission work throughout the world. Not only are baptisms recorded, but hours of time expended in publishing for every country in the world where the Jehovah's Witnesses are active.

Not surprisingly, the U.S. has the largest number of baptisms—more than 43,000. Mexico was second with 24,888, and Brazil a close third with 23,556. Brazil was more cost effective, however, having expended only 44 million hours of publishing in comparison to Mexico's 58 million. In Morocco, there were no baptisms, despite more than 9,000 hours of publishing. Italy, often considered a very difficult field of service for missionaries, reaped 12,676 baptisms as a result of somewhat more than 43 million hours of publishing.[8]

Some countries indicate surprising success for Jehovah's Witnesses. Japan, for example, is a very difficult field for Christian missionaries. In 1988, "membership of Protestant churches remained virtually unchanged at 99,300."[9] The Jehovah's Witnesses, however, reported more than 9,000 baptisms with more than 60 million hours.[10]

WORLDWIDE CHURCH OF GOD

Unlike the Mormons and Jehovah's Witnesses and most other nontraditional religious movements that have arisen over the past century, the Worldwide Church of God does not have a high-powered evangelistic or missionary program. The underlying rationale behind this lack of evangelism is theological in nature. According to the late Herbert W. Armstrong, "the purpose and function of the Church has been grossly misunderstood," and this misunderstanding has been the primary motivation for traditional evangelism and missionary outreach. "So let us clarify once for all time," he writes, "that the purpose of the Church is definitely not to preach or persuade the whole world into a spiritual salvation, now—before Christ's second coming!"[11]

Armstrong's position on missionary endeavors is not entirely unlike that of those churchmen who disputed with William Carey in the late eighteenth century when he was challenging his contemporaries to accept their responsibility in carrying out the Great Commission. They argued that the Great Commission was given to the Apostles who had opportunity to fulfill its directive in the first century. According to Armstrong, the "Great Commission to be sent forth with Christ's Gospel Message was given only to those who were apostles. . . . not the lay members of the Church," and not surprisingly, he viewed himself "God's apostle for our day."[12] The fulfilling of the Great Commission, then, is spreading the message of Herbert W. Armstrong through radio, television, and the printed word.

Armstrong began his worldwide outreach in the 1950s with a lecture tour to various cities in the British Isles. His following grew rapidly as his radio ministry expanded. By the end of that decade his radio messages had penetrated every continent, with more than four million listeners worldwide.[13]

The message of Herbert W. Armstrong, that reaches some one hundred and fifty million people through the printed page and the air waves, is certainly not a typical missionary message of evangelism or even doctrinal issues. It is a message to a world blinded by Satan, and the focus is on moral and family values or international affairs, although this message departs from the traditional Christian understanding of scriptural truths. "Millions have experienced changes in their marital lives through our broadcasts and through reading the instructional booklets and magazine articles," boasts a church publication. "From New Zealand to Africa, and from the Swiss Alps to Puget Sound, tens of thousands write of the deep and far reaching changes effected in their homes and families through a better understanding of God-revealed ways of right, clean, wholesome living."[14]

Another aspect of the Armstrong "missionary" outreach is that of recruiting students from abroad. Isaiah Issong, a young Nigerian, has testified how he was tempted and nearly enticed by the offer of a free American education: "Ambassador College has been an arm of Armstrong's dragnet. . . . Most of our Nigerian students who obtain their scholarships into the Ambassador College do not . . . realize that the Worldwide Church of God is never a true church of God. I would have been personally entrapped sometime in 1969 when there was a recruitment drive or a cry for willing young men to take the offer."[15]

THE WAY INTERNATIONAL

The Way International, another organization whose teaching departs from a traditional Christian understanding of Scripture, does not sponsor missionaries in the traditional sense of sending out trained professionals for lifetime ministries. Indeed, the organization has purposely avoided that method of evangelism for philosophical reasons. Correspondence from The Way College of Biblical Research in Rome City, Indiana, outlines the movement's concept of foreign missions:

We do not believe in missionary programs. We feel that the Word clearly states that every believer is responsible to speak God's Word and bring people to Christ. We are an international ministry, not because we have a mission program, but because our people so love God that they speak of Him wherever they go.

Most of the outreach in our sister countries has come in one of three ways. First, it comes from winning a foreign student in college in this country who goes home and takes the Word with him. Secondly, it comes from U.S. servicemen stationed overseas, speaking the Word in the course of their daily activities. Lastly, it comes from students who go and study abroad.[16]

But despite this disavowal of missionary activity, the movement sponsors WOW (Word Over the World) Ambassadors who conduct intensive evangelistic outreach much like Mormon missionaries do. They volunteer for one year of service, during which time they are required to meet their own expenses and return a tenth of their earnings back to the headquarters. In 1974, more than a thousand Ambassadors were commissioned to various regions of the United States, and in 1975, the number more than doubled. The projected goal was to commission more than two hundred thousand by 1985, and more than three million by 1990, goals that have had no bearing on reality.[17]

Some of the most successful evangelistic outreach in recent years has been realized overseas, where, according to the movement's own *Way Magazine*, the missionary activity has expanded greatly since the 1960s. As in the United States, this has been largely through the WOW arm of the movement. "The WOW Ambassador outreach worldwide has proven to be a great catalyst in reaching the world with God's Word and in raising up leadership among the believers."[18]

The vastness of this worldwide outreach is significant for such a relatively young organization. "From the southern port of Punta Arenas, Chile, to the northern gold fields of Fairbanks, Alaska— from the industrial city of Tokyo, Japan, to the small villages of Zaire, Africa—from the sprawling suburbs of Sydney, Australia, to the streets of Amsterdam—Word Over the World Ambassadors are living up to their name." The article goes on to say that "WOW Ambassadors are speaking God's Word on every continent of the world. These lay missionaries are natives not only of North America but of Third World countries as well." In 1985, "many South American . . . Ambassadors were commissioned in Colombia, Peru, Chile, and Argentina" and "in Africa, WOW Ambassadors are now serving in countries of Zaire, Angola, and the Congo." Indeed, in September of 1985 "Zaire commissioned over one thousand WOWs, to begin the fifth year of the program there."[19]

This worldwide outreach is based on founder Victor Paul Wierwille's strong emphasis on personal evangelism by every believer—an emphasis patterned after that of the early church and one that he maintains totally contradicts the missionary methodology of most denominations and mission organizations.

In two years and three months all Asia Minor heard the Word of God. In our day and time, with our multi-million dollars spent for foreign missions, publications, newspapers, radios, televisions and all other media, this event has never been repeated. We have never reached all Asia Minor with the Word of God in one generation. But the Apostle Paul and a handful of believers accomplished the feat in two years and three months. Either God has changed or Paul and those men who studied at the school of Tyrannus had tapped into something which they utilized to its capacity.[20]

THE UNIFICATION CHURCH

Since the first missionary was sent abroad in 1958, the Unification church—officially named The Holy Spirit Association for the Unification of World Christianity—has viewed missionary work as a top priority. Uniting people of all world religions is a central theme of the movement, and missionaries are the vehicle to bring about this one world religion under the leadership of Sun Myung Moon. In 1975, with missionaries already in more than thirty countries, Moon launched a worldwide blitz. It was a strange, if not utterly bizarre, foreign missionary program. Two hundred and sixty-three missionaries were commissioned to go to some one hundred countries to begin pioneer work. In most instances, the missionaries were sent in teams of three—an American, a Japanese, and a German—without any groundwork having been laid in the country to which they were assigned.[21]

Not surprisingly, there were many problems—particularly communication barriers between the missionaries themselves and between the missionaries and their target groups. The church has seen growth in some areas of the world such as Brazil and the Philippines, but the ideal of unifying all religions appeared to be doomed from the beginning.

In addition to its regular missionary outreach endeavors, the Unification church has a number of "mission" organizations that are not officially under the direct control of the church. The International Relief Friendship Foundation (IRFF) is an example. It was founded by church members for the purpose of church outreach, but it has remained a separate relief organization, which allows it to benefit from government funding for many of its projects. These projects have been conducted in some forty countries throughout the world and include such community needs as irrigation systems and elementary schools.[22]

But even though IRFF pretends to be simply a humanitarian organization, its agenda is blatantly one of promoting the teachings of the Unification church. An article in the July 1989 issue of *Unification News* told of a new primary school in Uganda that enrolls four hundred fifty children. The eighty-acre plot on which the school is built was donated by a local man, who probably had no knowledge of the doctrines of the UC. What are the objectives of the school? "1. To offer primary education in a rural area as a service to the nation and people of Uganda. 2. To improve the educational system by guiding children to be responsible as early as possible to live the Principle lifestyle. 3. To lay a foundation for a proposed polytechnical school." The teachers are mainly Africans, and they are expected to attend two-day and seven-day Principle workshops.[23]

One of the most recent missionary thrusts of the Unification church is focused on Mainland China. In March, 1990, the Fourth Southeast Asia Regional Conference convened in Bangkok, and there Rev. Kim, the Regional Director, challenged those present to bring the message of the Unification church to China through the Chinese who are in neighboring countries. "With the realization that . . . our common purpose is to restore China, all participants enthusiastically united immediately in order to fulfill this great mission."[24]

HARE KRISHNAS

Like the Way International and the Unification church, the Hare Krishnas have a worldwide evangelistic emphasis embodied in their name—officially known as the International Society for Krishna Consciousness. Unlike most forms of Hinduism, the Hare Krishna sect is a missionary movement that seeks to win converts from other religions. According to the movement's literature, "It is not recommended that a Krishna conscious devotee go into seclusion to chant by himself and thereby gain salvation for himself alone. Our duty and religious obligation is to go out into the streets where the people in general can hear the chanting and see the dancing."[25]

Like the Mormons, the Hare Krishnas are spreading their faith through the translation of their scripture. One such project has been the translation of Swami Prabhupada's *Bhagavad-gita As It Is* into Chinese. This volume contains the Hindu scripture with a commentary on each verse, and it is considered essential reading for the spread of Krishna consciousness. The potential value of having a Chinese translation is very great, according to the translator: "Although China and India are neighbors, very little of the rich spiritual tradition of India has penetrated China, largely because of the language barrier. Now that impediment has been removed—and the significance for the spiritual development of China cannot be overestimated."[26]

NEW AGE MOVEMENT

As is true of the contemporary cultic movements, the growth and expansion of the New Age movement and the occult has not been limited to North America. Europe has been particularly vulnerable to New Age and occultic practices—due in part to the decline of Christianity and the corresponding spiritual vacuum in society. A recent headline from West Germany illustrates this. A newspaper story entitled, "The Occult is Spreading in Our Schools," reports that as many as ten thousand teenagers are involved in such practices as seances, black sabbaths, devil worship, animal sacrifices, and experiments with pendulums. Said one source, "Their thoughts constantly revolve around the puzzling world of the spirits."[27]

In France, astrology is on the rise, and it is far more than just a curiosity. "To many it has become an infatuation. And to some a way of life. It is reported that eighty percent of the French people know their sign of the zodiac and seventy percent regularly read their horoscope." Indeed, "astrologers outnumber medical doctors in France by a five to three ratio." A weekday television game show features a "wheel of fortune sporting the twelve signs of the zodiac," and "heads of companies are turning to astrologers for advice." As in Germany, there is a spiritual vacuum to be filled, and New Age and occultic ideology is readily available to meet the need.[28]

HOME-GROWN CULTIC MOVEMENTS

In addition to the many American-based cultic movements that are thriving overseas, there are numerous pseudo-Christian cults that have captured the allegiance of millions of people. This is not a new phenomenon. Indeed, syncretistic movements that incorporate Christianity with other religions have frequently emerged in the wake of missionary outreach. In the 1830s, for example, the Worshippers of Shang-ti arose in China, through the preaching of Hung Xiu-quan, who had become familiar with Christianity through a tract written by a missionary. He testified to a series of visions, during which time he was taken on celestial visits to consult with bearded sages. From them he was instructed to destroy idols to appease God the Father and Jesus the Elder Brother. Hung and his cousin baptized themselves and then began to preach their new form of Christianity, which included ecstatic forms of prophesying, animal sacrifices, and the practice of polygamy.[29] Although there is no known connection, the movement has some amazing parallels with Mormonism, which also arose in the 1830s.

Today such movements continue to flourish. This is particularly true in Africa, where countless independent movements have arisen over the past century and more. According to an article in the *Nation*, a Nairobi newspaper, "Kenya has eight hundred registered sects, the highest in the world."[30] One such movement is led by the self-proclaimed prophetess Mary Akatsa, who claims that during one of her many visionary experiences with Jesus, he removed her tongue and gave her a new one with the instructions: "With this tongue you will speak my words. You will have power over all evil forces.... You will read people's problems as they will be written on their chests." In 1988, newspaper headlines read, "Did Jesus Visit Kawangware?," after Akatsa claimed that Jesus appeared in person before a large crowd at one of her open-air meetings.[31]

In the Philippines, the Inglesia Ni Cristo (Church of Christ) claims the allegiance of more than a million people, with a total worldwide membership of some three million. Though claiming to follow the precepts of the Bible, the movement is dominated by authoritarian leadership and insists that it alone is the true church and that no one can be saved apart from the organization.[32]

In Peru, a cultic movement known as the New Covenant Israelites numbers some sixty thousand and continues to expand as new members—motivated by fear of a coming disaster—join communal centers located in the mountains and jungles. "Israelite men grow their hair long and wear beards in the style of orthodox Jews.... They also offer animal sacrifices for sin and keep Jewish feasts, especially the Passover. In weekly services they claim to frequently speak in what they say are tongues given by the Holy Spirit, receive visions, and sometimes claim to float in the air." A substantial portion of their growth is attained through typical cultic fashion; they "infiltrate small Evangelical churches in order to gain converts for their group."[33]

CONCLUSION

Yes, *the cults are coming*, but equally significant is the fact that *the cults are going*. This reality ought to be of paramount concern to churches who are sending missionaries abroad and who are seeking to financially assist mission agencies based in the non-Western world. Cultic movements win most of their converts not from unreached people groups or from other world religions, but from Christian churches—often among Christians who are not well founded in biblical doctrine and the beliefs and tactics of cults.

It is imperative that prospective missionaries and non-Western church leaders be aware of growth and international expansion of cultic movements and that they be involved in educating lay Christians about the dangers of false doctrine and in training them to respond effectively.

Above all, Christians worldwide must realize that their battle against false cults is not lost. The continued rapid expansion of cults is not inevitable, as has been shown to be true in Zaire. After visiting the U.S. in 1985, Raphael Etsea, the vice president of Zaire Africa Inland Church, was more determined than ever to seek to slow the growth of the Jehovah's Witnesses in his country. He was troubled that all too often his people accept at face value what they hear from religious teachers from the West, and he vowed to make his people more aware of cultic movements.

Since 1985, Zaire has seen a slowed growth of Jehovah's Witnesses. The 1986 *Yearbook* (containing statistics for 1985) reported 5,573 baptisms, while the 1989 *Yearbook* reports only 1705. The numbers are significant—especially considering the number of publishing hours expended. In 1985, nearly eleven million hours were expended, but in 1988, with only thirty percent of the baptisms, there were nearly ten million hours (or ninety percent of the hours). This could happen all over the world if we would redouble our efforts to counter the cults and properly educate Christian believers.

Chapter Notes

Introduction

1. Stanley Hauerwas, "Self-Sacrifice as Demonic: A Theological Response to Jonestown," in *Violence and Religious Commitment,* ed. Ken Levi (University Park: the Pennsylvania State University Press, 1982), 159.
2. Hauerwas, 160.
3. Hauerwas, 191.
4. Ronald M. Enroth and J. Gordon Melton, *Why Cults Succeed Where the Church Fails* (Elgin, Illinois: Brethren Press, 1985), 126.
5. *Unification News* (January 1990), 11.
6. *Unification News* (January 1990), 8.
7. *Unification News* (December 1989), 11.
8. *Unification News* (December 1989), 9.
9. Ronald Enroth, *The Lure of the Cults & New Religions* (Downers Grove, Illinois: InterVarsity Press, 1987), 35.
10. David Fetcho, "Disclosing the Unknown God: Evangelism to the New Religions," *Update,* December 1982, 8.
11. Fetcho, 10.

THREE
The New Age

1. Rick Fields and others, *Chop Wood, Carry Water: A Guide to Finding Spiritual Fulfillment in Everyday Life* (Los Angeles, CA: Jeremy P. Tarcher, 1984), xii.
2. Fields, *Chop Wood, Carry Water,* xiv.
3. Paul McGuire, *Evangelizing the New Age* (Ann Arbor, MI: Servant Publications, 1989), 139.
4. Francis Schaeffer, *Christian Manifesto* (Westchester, IL: Crossway, 1981), 17.
5. See my *Integrative Theology* (Grand Rapids: Zondervan, 1987), Vol. 1 chapter 2; and my *Decide for Yourself: A Theological Workbook* (Downers Grove, IL: InterVarsity Press, 1970), chapter 1.
6. See my "Why I Talk with New Agers," *Christian Research Journal* 12:1 (Summer 1989), 7.

7. Marilyn Ferguson, *The Aquarian Conspiracy: Personal and Social Transformation in the 1980s* (Los Angeles, CA: Jeremy P. Tarcher, 1980).

8. Robert N. Bellah, et al., *Habits of the Heart* (New York: Harper and Row, 1985), 355.

9. McGuire, 88.

10. McGuire, 34.

11. Elliot Miller, letter to Gordon Lewis, May 13, 1989.

12. Elliot Miller, *A Crash Course in the New Age Movement* (Grand Rapids, MI: Baker, 1989), Appendix D, 215-216. (For the rest of the story see pages 211-223.)

13. Christian Research Institute, Box 500, San Juan Capistrano, CA 92693-0500.

14. Lausanne Covenant, 1974.

15. For a contrast of the New Age myths with the historicity of the resurrection, see Kerry D. McRoberts, *New Age or Old Lie?* (Peabody, MA: Hendrickson, 1989). For more extensive support for Christ's resurrection and its theological significance see my *Integrative Theology*, vol. 2, chapter 4.

16. Gordon R. Lewis, *Confronting the Cults* (Phillipsburg, NJ: Presbyterian and Reformed, 1966).

17. Gordon R. Lewis, *What Everyone Should Know About Transcendental Meditation* (Glendale, CA: Regal, 1975). Now available only from the author at Denver Seminary, Denver, CO 80210.

18. Gordon Lewis and Bruce Demarest, *Integrative Theology* (Grand Rapids, MI: Zondervan, Vol. 1 1987; Vol. 2 March, 1990).

19. For a theology that interacts with contemporary alternatives including doctrines and practices of the New Age movement see Gordon Lewis and Bruce Demarest, *Integrative Theology* (Grand Rapids, MI: Zondervan, 1987).

20. For additional help with apologetics see Conlin Chapman, *The Case for Christianity* (Grand Rapids, MI: Eerdmans, 1981); Gordon Lewis, *Testing Christianity's Truth Claims* (1976, write author, Denver Seminary, Box 10,000, Denver, CO 80210); Norman Geisler, *Worlds Apart* (Grand Rapids, MI: Baker, 1989); John P. Newport, *Life's Ultimate Questions* (Dallas, TX: Word, 1989); James W. Sire, *The Universe Next Door* (Downers Grove, IL: InterVarsity Press, 1988).

21. For challenging works on the filling of the Spirit ("baptism" of the Spirit aside), see Paul McGuire, *Supernatural Faith in the New Age* (Springdale, PA: Whitaker, 1987; and Paul McGuire, *Evangelizing the New Age* (Ann Arbor, MI: Servant Publications, 1989).

22. Edward R. Dayton, *That Everyone May Hear: Reaching the Unreached* (Monrovia, CA: MARC, 1979), 22.

FOUR
The Unification Church

1. Moon, "Causa Seminar Speech," August 29, 1985, 7-8. The *Unification News* (October 1985) report on this speech makes no mention of this claim, while the version of the speech in *Today's World* (October-November, 1985) gives different wording at this point. Since 1976 Rev. Moon's sermons are translated into English under the series title "Rev. Sun Myung Moon Speaks On." His earlier sermons went under the general title "Master Speaks." For bibliographical information, refer to Michael L. Mickler, *The Unification Church in America* (New York: Garland, 1987).

2. For information on the battles surrounding the Unification church consult David Bromley and Anson Shupe, Jr., *"Moonies" in America* (Beverly Hills: Sage, 1979); Mose Durst, *To Bigotry, No Sanction* (Chicago: Regnery Gateway, 1984); John T. Biermans, *The Odyssey of New Religions Today* (Toronto: Edwin Mellen, second edition, 1988).

3. This essay will use both Moonie and Unificationist interchangeably and neither term is meant in a pejorative fashion. Though Joy Irvine Garratt, public relations director for the Unification church in America, complained that *Christianity Today* magazine used the term "Moonie" to describe members of the Unification church, Rev. Moon uses the term often in his messages. Further, he predicted it was to be a word of honor by 1981. (See Garratt's letter to the editor, *Chistianity Today* April 19, 1985, 51, and Moon, "Critical Turning Point in the Dispensation of God," December 31, 1978, 13.)

4. *Victory for Freedom* (Washington: Committee to Defend the U.S. Constitution, 1985), 119. Many scholars have given almost boundless praise to Moon. For example, Richard Rubenstein has called Rev. Moon "a religious leader of preeminent significance . . . a man of genuine inspiration." Those who studied under Karl Barth and Paul Tillich could only be interpreters of other men's inspiration, he goes on to say, adding that "we could never become what the Rev. Moon is, a man of genuine inspiration capable of infusing others with his inspiration" (*Unification News* 1,1, February 22, 1982; 10).

5. For material on the life of Rev. Moon, see Frederick Sontag, *Sun Myung Moon and the Unification Church* (Nashville, Abingdon, 1977), 70-96, and three speeches by Moon on "History of the Unification Church" (December 27, 28, 29, 1971).

6. Kim died on September 30, 1989. For her testimony about Rev. Moon, see *Unification News* (November and December, 1989). On a more academic level consult her *Unification Theology* (New York: HWA-UWC, 1987, second edition).

7. See *Introduction of the CAUSA Worldview* (New York: HSA-UWC, 1985). For concerns about Moon's political activities, note David G. Racer, Jr., *Not For Sale* (St. Paul: Tiny Press, 1989).

8. On the Washington newspaper, see, for example, Timothy Noah, "Paper Moon," *The New Republic* (July 19 and 26, 1982), 16-18. On financial matters, consult David Bromley, "Economic Structure of the Unificationist Movement," *Journal for the Scientific Study of Religion* 24, 3 (September 1985), 253-274.

9. The church reproduced the interview from the Russian newspaper *Abroad* as an advertisement in *The New York Times* (December 3, 1989).

10. *Divine Principle* (5th ed., 1977), p. 16.

11. *Divine Principle* offers an extreme form of dispensationalism in its showing that both Old Testament history and history since Christ can be divided into equal and parallel sections, culminating in a different Messiah for the two main eras.

12. See Won Pil Kim, "Testimony of Father's Life," (October 14, 1979), 27-28.

13. As one example of Moon's incredible claims in this regard, note the following self-evaluation: "Before I came the universe was engulfed in darkness. All the many philosophers and religious people knew nothing of the heart of God and the meaning of the Bible. . . . Noah, Abraham, Moses, all the Old Testament prophets, John the Baptist and even Jesus' mission all ended in failure. In my own lifetime I have to mend everything and replace all those past failures with success." Moon, "The 23rd Anniversary of the Unification Church and the History of God's Dispensation," (May 1, 1977), 11-12.

14. On the concept of indemnity, see *Divine Principle*, 222-227, and the essays in Deane William Ferm, ed. *Restoring the Kingdom* (New York: Paragon, 1984).

15. Moon is known as True Father and his wife as True Mother. Moonies pray in the name of these True Parents, though they would also pray in the name of Jesus. Moon refers to the year of his marriage as the turning point in history. See *Master Speaks* (December 22, 1971), 4.

16. For Moon's statements see his sermons of January 2, 1980 (p. 8), January 2, 1977 (p. 6), and January 13, 1980 (p. 9).

17. For details on these rituals see the book *The Tradition* (New York: HSA: UWC, 1985). The Unification view of sex and marriage is discussed in Joseph Fichter, *The Holy Family of Father Moon* (Kansas City: Leaven Press, 1985), James H. Grace, *Sex and Marriage in the Unification Movement* (New York: Edwin Mellen, 1985), and Gene G. James, ed., *The Family and the Unification Church* (New York: Rose of Sharon Press, 1983).

18. Richard Quebedeux offers this testimony of the loving reality of the Unification church: "I have found in the living example of Moonies, of

Unification people, something I never found, quite frankly, anywhere else" (Today's World, 5, 4 April 1984, 36).

19. Testimony from a Unification member in Dallas, Texas, sent to this author in preparation for his lecture "Wife of the Lord: The Role of Mrs. Moon in the Unification Church," given at the Annual Meeting, American Academy of Religion, Anaheim, CA., November 1989. See also the testimonies of Moonies collected in Joseph Fichter, *Autobiographies of Confession* (New York: Edwin Mellen, 1987).

20. For Moon's theories see his sermon "The Participants in Celebrating Christmas," December 25, 1977.

21. See Moon's sermon "The Spirit World and Physical World," February 6, 1977, 14, for example.

22. For documentation, see Moon's sermons of August 1, 1976, p. 10; September 20, 1976, p. 5; February 23, 1977, p. 11; October 3, 1976, p. 15; May 20, 1984, p. 11; and February 27, 1977, p. 15.

23. On Heung Jin Nim see Moon's sermons of February 7, 1984, p. 9; May 1, 1984, pp. 13-14; and Today's World 5 (January-February 1984, and April 1984).

SIX
The Occult

1. Joseph M. Murphy, *Santeria: An African Religion in America* (Boston: Beacon Press, 1988), 130.

2. Daniel Lawrence O'Keefe, *Stolen Lightning: the Social Theory of Magic* (New York: Continuum Publishing Co., 1982), 540.

3. Arthur Versluis, *The Egyptian Mysteries* (London: Arkana Press, 1988), 158 (note 27).

4. *The Litany of Ra,* Ch. IV, 1, as cited in ibid., 158.

5. In many ways it is easier to witness to a black magician than to a dyed-in-the-wool naturalist who pursues his autonomy by denying the supernatural and repressing his human need for a relationship to it. That repression is what causes his ideas—such as materialism, secular humanism, and scientism—to function for him in such a peculiarly religious manner.

6. For an excellent account of this, see: Mark Mittleberg, "Implementing Apologetics in the Local Church," *Contend for the Faith: Collected Papers of the Rockford Conference on Discernment and Evangelism,* Eric Pement, Ed. (Chicago: Cornerstone Press), *Evangelical Ministries to New Religions* (Chicago: 1990).

7. D.A. Carson, *Biblical Interpretation and the Church: the Problem of Contextualization* (Nashville: Thomas Nelson Pub., 1984), 141-143.

SEVEN
Jehovah's Witnesses

1. "Carefully Following the Orders of the King," Summer 1985 Integrity Keepers District Convention of Jehovah's Witnesses.
2. *The Watchtower*, February 15, 1983, 12.
3. *The Watchtower*, November 15, 1981, 21.
4. *The Watchtower*, December 1, 1981, 27.
5. *The Watchtower*, January 15, 1983, 22.
6. *Yearbook*, January, 1990. (Brooklyn, NY: Watchtower Bible and Tract Society, 1990), inside cover.
7. *Yearbook*, 1990, inside cover.
8. Jehovah's Witnesses refer to themselves as Jehovah's *witnesses*.
9. *Let God Be True* (New York: Watchtower Bible and Tract Society, Inc., 1946), 213.
10. Volume Seven was published after Russell's death, from his unpublished notes and drafts of the work.
11. *The Watchtower*, September 15, 1910, 298.
12. Some of their failed dates for Armageddon include 1874, 1914, 1918, 1925, 1942, and 1975. For more information on the false prophecies of the Watchtower, see Edmund Gruss' *Jehovah's Witnesses and Prophetic Speculation* (Nutley, NJ: Presbyterian and Reformed Publishing Company, 1972).
13. *The Watchtower*, December 1, 1984, 16-18.
14. All verses quoted are from *The Holy Bible, New King James Version* (Nashville, TN: Thomas Nelson, Inc., 1982).
15. For a discussion of these views and a biblical evaluation, see Bob and Gretchen Passantino, *Answers to the Cultist at Your Door* (Eugene, OR: Harvest House Publishers, 1981), 55-60.
16. Quoted from the Jehovah's Witness translation *The New World Translation* (New York: Watchtower Bible and Tract Society, 1961).
17. *Reasoning from the Scriptures* (Brooklyn, NY: Watchtower Bible and Tract Society, 1985), 17.
18. *Reasoning*, 424.
19. For discussion on these two misunderstandings, see *Answers to the Cultist*, 65, 66.
20. See, for example, "The Doctrine of the Trinity," by James Oliver Buswell, Jr., in *A Systematic Theology of the Christian Religion* (Grand Rapids, MI: Zondervan Publishing House, 1962), 102-129.
21. Further discussion on the personality and deity of the Holy Spirit is in *Answers to the Cultist*, 74-76.
22. *Reasoning*, 209.
23. *The New World Translation*.

24. See, for example, "Resolving the Debate," a discussion of the translation and linguistics of John 1:1, by Eugene H. Glassman in *The Translation Debate: What Makes a Translation Good?* (Downers Grove, IL: InterVarsity Press, 1981), 93-96; E.C. Colewell's "A Definite Rule for the Use of the Article in the Greek New Testament," *Journal of Biblical Literature,* 1933; Philip B. Harner's "Qualitative Anarthrous Predicate Nouns: Mark 15:39 and John 1:1" in *Journal of Biblical Literature,* 92, 1, (March 1973), 75-87; also Harner's *The "I Am" of the Fourth Gospel: A Study in Johannine Usage and Thought* (Philadelphia: Fortress Press, 1970); Daniel B. Wallace's "The Semantics and Exegetical Significance of the Object Complement Construction in the New Testament," *Grace Theological Journal,* Vol. 6, No. 1, (1985), 91-112; C. Kuehne's "The Greek Article and the Doctrine of Christ's Deity," *Journal of Theology (Church of the Lutheran Confession)* Vol. 13, Nos. 3, 4, and Vol. 14, Nos. 1-4, (1973 and 1974); and "Colossians 1:15-20: An Early Christian Hymn Celebrating the Lordship of Christ," Paul Beasley-Murray, in *Pauline Studies,* edited by Donald A. Hagner and Murray J. Harris, (Grand Rapids, MI: William B. Eerdmans Publishing Company, 1980), 169-183.
25. See Beasley-Murray and Wallace.
26. The brackets are in the New World Translation.
27. See, for example, the Septuagint Greek translation of Exodus 4:22.
28. See "The Incarnation and Logic: Their Compatibility Defended," by Norman L. Geisler and William D. Watkins, *Trinity Journal,* no. 6, (1985), 185-197.
29. *Let God Be True,* 272.
30. *Reasoning,* 217.
31. *Reasoning,* 333.
32. *Reasoning,* 333.
33. *Reasoning,* 217, 218.
34. John 8:24, literally, "I am," although most translations read "I am *he.*"
35. See Paul's example in Acts 17:2, 3, 17-34.
36. For a good introduction to the controversial subject of mind control or "brainwashing," I recommend a short summary (with recommendations of other sources) by and on the differences between cultic and Christian conversion, see James T. Richardson, "Conversion, Brainwashing, and Deprogramming in New Religions," and James Bjornstad, "Cultic and Christian Conversion: Is There a Difference?" in *New Religious Movements Update,* Vol. 6, No. 1, (March 1982), 34-49 and 50-64.
37. "Apologetics" means the discipline of giving a reasonable defense for one's beliefs.
38. For apologetics, see 1 Peter 3:15, for biblical counseling, see Exodus 18:13-27, and for loving commitment, see James 2:14-16.

EIGHT
The Unity School of Christianity

1. Charles Fillmore, The Science of Being and Christian Healing (Kansas City: Unity Tract Society, 1912), 256.
2. Eric Butterworth, Unity: A Quest for Truth (New York: Robert Speller & Sons, Publishers, Inc., 1956), 23.
3. Marcus Bach, The Unity Way of Life (Englewood Cliffs, NJ: Prentice-Hall, 1962), 163.
4. James D. Freeman, The Household of Faith (Lees Summit, MO: Unity School of Christianity, 1951), 41
5. Butterworth, 9.
6. Freeman, 27
7. Freeman, 57.
8. Butterworth, 21.
9. The Daily Word is often confused with a legitimate Christian publication Our Daily Bread (Radio Bible Class, Grand Rapids, MI). Our Daily Bread is based upon the Bible from a Reformed tradition.
10. Charles Fillmore, Metaphysical Bible Dictionary (Lees Summit, MO: Unity School Of Christianity, 1931), 332.
11. Clark Pinnock, Biblical Revelation (Chicago: Moody, 1971), 210.
12. Butterworth, 37.
13. Fillmore, Science of Being, 230 and Metaphysical Bible Dictionary, 151.
14. Fillmore, Metaphysical Bible Dictionary, 2.
15. Fillmore, Science of Being, 29.
16. Fillmore, Metaphysical Bible Dictionary, 4.
17. Butterworth, 16.
18. Fillmore, Science of Being, 15.
19. H. Emilie Cady, Lessons in Truth (Lees Summit, MO: Unity School Of Christianity, 1926), 6, 11.
20. Norman Geisler, Christian Apologetics (Grand Rapids: Baker Book House, 1976).
21. Cady, Lessons in Truth, 9.
22. Ibid, p. 9.
23. H. Emilie Cady, God a Present Help (Lees Summit, MO: Unity Books, 1938), 52-53.
24. Fillmore, Science of Being, 8.
25. Fillmore, 22.
26. Fillmore, Science of Being, 19, and Fillmore, Metaphysical Bible Dictionary, 629.
27. Fillmore, Science of Being, 345.
28. Fillmore, Science of Being, 150.
29. Unity magazine (Lees Summit, MO: Unity School of Christianity, Vol. 14, 1901), 149.

30. Fillmore, *Metaphysical Bible Dictionary*, 629.
31. c.f., Josh McDowell, *Evidence That Demands a Verdict* (Arrowhead Springs, CA: Here's Life, 1985).
32. Fillmore, *Science of Being*, 7.
33. Cady, *Lessons in Truth*, 7.
34. Fillmore, *Metaphysical Bible Dictionary*, 349.
35. Fillmore, *Science of Being*, 56.
36. Fillmore, *Metaphysical Bible Dictionary*, 79.
37. Fillmore, *Metaphysical Bible Dictionary*, 129.
38. Frank B. Whitney, *Mightier Than Circumstance* (Kansas City, MO: Unity School of Christianity, 1943), 146.
39. Fillmore, *Science of Being*, 24; and Imelda O. Shanklin, *Selected Studies* (Kansas City, MO: Unity School of Christianity, 1926), 17.
40. Fillmore, *Science of Being*, 35.
41. Fillmore, *Metaphysical Bible Dictionary*, 349.
42. Fillmore, *Science of Being*, 175.
43. Freeman, 167.
44. Butterworth, 15.

NINE
Scientology

1. *Time* (April 5, 1976), 57.
2. *Time* (February 10, 1986), 86.
3. *Publisher's Weekly* (September 16, 1950), 1124.
4. L. Ron Hubbard, *Dianetics: A Modern Science of Mental Health* (Los Angeles: Bridge Publications, Inc. 1986), 7.
5. *Dianetics*, 14.
6. *Dianetics*, 26.
7. *Dianetics*, 26, 29, 81, 56.
8. *Dianetics*, 61.
9. *Dianetics*, 577.
10. *Dianetics*, 56.
11. *Dianetics*, 82.
12. *Dianetics*, 84.
13. *Dianetics*, 122, 125, 228.
14. *Dianetics*, 17, 18.
15. L. Ron Hubbard, *Dianetics: A Modern Science of Mental Health* (New York: Hermitage House, 1950), xix.
16. Isaac Asimov, *In Memory Yet Green* (Garden City, NJ: Doubleday & Company, Inc., 1979), 654.
17. *Time* (September 3, 1951), 51.
18. Martin Gardner, *Fads and Fallacies in the Name of Science* (New York: Dover Publications, Inc., 1958), 270.

19. Paul Sann, *Fads, Fallacies, and Delusions of the American People* (New York: Crown Publishers, 1967), 115.

20. *Christianity Today* (September 17, 1982), 33.

21. L. Ron Hubbard, *Scientology: A History of Man* (Los Angeles: American St. Hill Organization, 1968), 7.

22. Paulette Cooper, *The Scandal of Scientology* (New York: Tower Publishing, Inc., 1971), 147.

23. *Time* (September 3, 1951), 51.

24. L. Ron Hubbard, *The Phoenix Lectures* (Los Angeles: American St. Hill Organization, 1968), 12.

25. *The Phoenix Lectures*, 16.

26. *The Phoenix Lectures*, 18.

27. *The Phoenix Lectures*, 19.

28. *Advance!* (December, 1974), 5.

29. L. Ron Hubbard, *Volunteer Minister's Handbook* (Los Angeles: Church of Scientology, 1976), xiv.

30. Anonymous, *Hubbard: Ceremonies of the Founding Church of Scientology* (Sussex, England: The Publications Organization Worldwide, 1967), 73.

31. L. Ron Hubbard, *Scientology 8-8008* (Los Angeles: ASHO, 1967), 73.

32. Hubbard, *The Phoenix Lectures*, 3.

33. Kevin Victor Anderson, *The Victoria Report of the Board of Inquiry into Scientology* (Melbourne, Australia: A.C. Brooks, Gov't. Printer, 1965), 151.

34. *The Phoenix Lectures*, 31.

35. L. Ron Hubbard, *Scientology Clear Procedure, Issue One* (Los Angeles: ASHO, 1969), 21.

36. Hubbard, *History of Man*, 38.

37. *The Victoria Report of the Board of Inquiry into Scientology*, 150.

38. *Volunteer Minister's Handbook*, 551.

39. L. Ron Hubbard, *Scientology: Self-Analysis* (Los Angeles: ASHO, 1974), 19.

40. L. Ron Hubbard, *Scientology: A World Religion Emerges in the Space Age* (Los Angeles: Church of Scientology, 1974), 15.

41. *The Phoenix Lectures*, 27.

42. L. Ron Hubbard, *Science of Survival*, Book 2 (Los Angeles: ASHO, 1973), 255.

43. Norman Geisler and J. Yuako Amano, *The Reincarnation Sensation* (Wheaton: Tyndale Publishers, 1986). This book deals very well with reincarnation from a Christian perspective. Chapters four and five challenge the types of supposed recalls people have of former lives.

44. Kurt Van Gorden, *Why Christians Believe in the Resurrection* (Orange, CA: Jude 3 Missions, 1987), 4. This Bible study on the resurrection and Jesus is available through Jude 3 Missions, P.O. Box 1901, Orange, CA 92668.

TEN
Confronting the Cults

1. Etienne P. Vanaa, "French Polynesia Region: Highlights for the '80s," *Saints Herald* (March 1982), 11.
2. John Ahmanson, *Secret History: A Translation of Vor Tids Muhamed*, trans. by Gleason L. Archer (Chicago: Moody, 1984), 16, 18.
3. Ruth A. Tucker, "Foreign Missionaries With a False Message," *Evangelical Missions Quarterly* (October 1984), 329.
4. James Warner and Styne M. Slade, *The Mormon Way* (Englewood Cliffs, NJ: Prentice Hall, 1976), 122, 130.
5. R. Lanier Britsch, "Mormon Missions: An Introduction to the Latter-day Saints Missionary System," *Occasional Bulletin* (January 1979), 23.
6. Ruth A. Tucker, "Nonorthodox Sects Report Global Membership Gains," *Christianity Today* (June 13, 1986), 50; interview with Mormon missionaries, September 1989.
7. Kenneth Woodward, "Onward Mormon Soldiers," *Newsweek* (April 17, 1981), 88.
8. *1989 Yearbook of Jehovah's Witnesses* (New York: Watchtower Bible and Tract Society, 1989), 34-41.
9. Melville Szto, "Church Planting in Japan," *Asian Mission* (September 1989), 3.
10. *1989 Yearbook*, 36.
11. Herbert W. Armstrong, *The Incredible Human Potential* (Pasadena: Worldwide Church of God, 1978), 114.
12. Armstrong, 114-120.
13. Joseph Hopkins, *The Armstrong Empire: A Look at the Worldwide Church of God* (Grand Rapids: Eerdmans, 1974), 51.
14. *This Is the Worldwide Church of God* (Pasadena: Worldwide Church of God, 1979), 21.
15. Isaiah A. Issong, "The Missionary Outreach of the Worldwide Church of God in Nigeria," Unpublished paper, Grand Rapids School of the Bible and Music, May 16, 1983, 4.
16. Correspondence from Wayne Clapp to Jimel Aumann, Grand Rapids, Michigan, March 22, 1983.
17. J.L. Williams, *Victor Paul Wierwille and The Way International* (Chicago: Moody, 1979), 38-39.
18. "International WOW Scene," *The Way Magazine* (November-December 1985), 31.
19. Ibid, p. 31.
20. Victor Paul Wierwille, *Power for Abundant Living* (New Knoxville, Ohio: The Way International, 1971), 109.

21. Chung Hwan Kwak, "World Missions," *Today's World* (May, 1983), 24.
22. "Serving the Needy: IRFF Projects Around the World," *Today's World* (July 1983), 26-29.
23. Ruth Robinson, "IRFF Teaching Health Care to Kampala's Poor," *Unification News* (July 1989), 12.
24. Ursula McLackland, "Building a Bridge to Mainland China," *Unification News* (May 1989), 10.
25. *The Krishna Consciousness Handbook* (March 24, 1970-March 12, 1971), 108-109.
26. "Govinda's Restaurant in Teheran: 'Down to Earth and Up to God,' " *Back to Godhead* (June 1981), 19.
27. "W. German Youth Turning to Occult, Authorities Warn," *Grand Rapids Press* (November 17, 1988), B4.
28. Marlene Kornbau, "Astrology in France: Fad or Fetter?," *Global Times* (January 1989), 1.
29. Stephen Neill, *A History of Christian Missions* (New York: Penguin, 1964), 286-288.
30. Daniel Kamanga, "Chaos in the Name of God," *Nation* (December 9, 1987), 13.
31. Nyaga wa Muto and Ben Mitukaa, "Did Jesus Visit Kawangware?," *Sunday Times* (Kenya), (June 26, 1988), 17.
32. Robert Elliff, *The Only True Church?* (published by Robert Elliff, 1989), *passim.*
33. "Peruvian Cult Gaining Members," *Christian Mission* (November-December 1989), 8.

Bibliography

ONE
Hinduism

Albrecht, Mark C. *Reincarnation.* Downers Grove, IL: InterVarsity Press, 1982, 1987.

Bharati, Agehenanda. *The Ochre Robe.* New York: Doubleday and Co., 1970.

Brown, W. Norman. *Man in the Universe: Some Continuities in Indian Thought.* Berkeley: University of California Press, 1970.

Radhakrishnan & Moore. *A Sourcebook in Indian Philosophy.* Princeton, NJ: Princeton University Press, 1957.

van Buitenen, J.A.B. *The Bhagavadgita in the Mahabharata.* Chicago: University of Chicago Press, 1981.

Yogananda, Paramahansa. *Autobiography of a Yogi.* London: Rider & Co., 1969.

Zaehner, R.C. *Hinduism.* London: Oxford University Press, 1962.

TWO
Buddhism

Conze, Edward, ed. *Buddhist Texts Through the Ages.* New York: Harper Torchbooks, 1964.

Kalupahana, David J. *Buddhist Philosophy: A Historical Analysis.* Honolulu: The University Press of Hawaii, 1976.

Layman, Emma McCloy. *Buddhism in America.* Chicago: Nelson-Hall, 1976.

Muck, Terry. *Alien Gods on American Turf.* Wheaton, IL: Victor Books, 1990.

Neill, Stephen. *Christian Faith and Other Religions.* London: Oxford University Press, 1970.

Rahula, Walpola. *What the Buddha Taught.* New York: Grove Press, 1974.

Saunders, E. Dale. *Buddhism in Japan.* Philadelphia: University of Pennsylvania Press, 1971.

Snellgrove, David, and Hugh Richardson. *A Cultural History of Tibet.* Boulder: Prajna Press, 1980.

Yamamoto, J. Isamu. *Beyond Buddhism: A Basic Introduction to the Buddhist Tradition.* Downers Grove: InterVarsity Press, 1982.

195

Other Books of Interest
by Servant Publications

The Power of the Gospel Invades the New Age Movement
Paul McGuire

Lured by the promise of spiritual power, healing, and a richer, more rewarding way of life, millions of people have become ensnared by age-old superstitions. Tragically, few voices have raised a call to evangelize those involved in the New Age religions.

Evangelizing the New Age takes you a step beyond other books by exposing the intense spiritual battle between the New Age and the kingdom of God. Paul McGuire explains how you can help your friends, neighbors, colleagues, and family members who are caught up in the New Age. Here is practical guidance for sharing the life-giving message of Christ in a way that will capture the imagination of modern men and women. *$7.95*

The Believer's Guide to Spiritual Warfare
Wising Up to Satan's Influence in Your World
Thomas B. White

As an expert in the field of spiritual warfare, Tom White has equipped thousands of men and women to discern and combat demonic forces in their world. *The Believer's Guide to Spiritual Warfare* offers biblically sound, accurate, and balanced teaching on the unseen war being waged around us.

Complete with real-life illustrations, sample prayers, proven techniques, and answers to the most commonly asked questions about warfare, this book will help believers to fulfill a central call of the gospel—to resist evil with the power and authority of the cross. *$8.95*